BRAIN GAMES

CROSSWORD PUZZLES

LARGE PRINT

Publications International, Ltd.

Puzzle Contributors: Kelly Clark, Mark Danna, Harvey Estes, Alun Evans, Ray Hamel, Timothy Park

Illustrators: Helem An, Shozen Jay Sato, Shavan R. Spears

ISBN-13: 978-1-4127-7761-2
ISBN-10: 1-4127-7761-5

Manufactured in U.S.A.

8 7 6 5 4 3 2 1

Easy on the Eyes, Not on the Brain

Crossword puzzles should be fun yet challenging—challenging on the brain, that is. If you'd like to give your eyes a break while still enjoying the mental workout only a challenging crossword can provide, *Brain Games®: Large Print Crossword Puzzles* is for you.

This book is loaded with more than 80 puzzles of varying difficulty, starting with easier puzzles and moving on to difficult ones that will really work your mental muscle. Each crossword puzzle is spread over two pages and printed in a readable type so you can challenge your brain—not your eyes—as you work each one.

You'll laugh (or groan) at silly puns sprinkled among the clues and scratch your head at how *that* theme relates to *those* clues—all while your cerebral muscles work like they've never worked before. And if you come across a clue you just can't figure out, puzzle answers are conveniently located in order in the back of the book.

So sit down, relax, and reenergize your brain by opening up *Brain Games®: Large Print Crossword Puzzles* today!

Zoo Story

ACROSS

1. Former Cleveland pitcher Charles
5. Phony
9. Belch
13. Yearly record
15. Britishism: 2 wds.
16. Song for Bartoli
17. Creepy person: 4 wds.
20. Chapeau
21. Collect patiently
22. Arctic quarter
23. Pitcher
24. "Strangers ___ Train": 2 wds.
25. Chicken: 2 wds.
30. Mad scientist's assistant
34. Dance in a line
35. Believer: suf.
36. Famous fiddler
37. The Greatest
38. Street swine: 2 wds.
42. Collar
43. Father of Portnoy
45. Fifties' initials
46. Lenya
48. Lady of the haus: Ger.
49. Overnight stars, in a way: 2 wds.
52. Appliance store items: abbr.
54. Regatta sights
55. Tend to the turkey
58. Domineering
60. Auto club initials
63. Relatives of the paparazzi: 2 wds.
66. The Shah's former country
67. Theater award
68. Sideshow attraction
69. Cereal grains
70. Max Jr. or Sr.
71. La Douce

DOWN

1. "Candy is dandy…" author
2. Magnani
3. No-see-um
4. Asian bovine
5. Sunday best
6. Powell-Loy costar
7. Late comedic actor Madeline
8. The mind's ___
9. Basement find
10. Mountain range
11. Rice: Ital.
12. El ___
14. Stockings, e.g.
18. "___ Three Lives": 2 wds.
19. Cheever's "The Sorrows of ___"
23. Work unit
24. von Bismarck
25. What you place around your neck
26. Tint
27. Loos or Ekberg
28. Fall drink
29. Ember
31. Ladies' escorts, for short
32. Speak
33. Kimonos
39. Tout's figures
40. Nabokov novel
41. "That's the story of, that's the ___ love": 2 wds.
44. Jim and Tim
47. Conjunctions
50. Blessed by the rabbi
51. Corned beef seconds
53. Relax; do nothing: sl.
55. TV's Chachi
56. Air
57. Sports fig.
58. Rum cake
59. Ron Howard role
60. Biblical name
61. First fellow
62. ___ silly question…: 2 wds.
64. Reiner
65. Site of the William Tell legend

Answers on page 172.

Lip Service

ACROSS

1. "Yikes"
5. Lumberyard tools
9. "Hungarian Rhapsodies" composer Franz
14. Employee's move, for short
15. "___ Silver! Away!"
16. "…an old woman who lived in ___ ___"
17. Comfy footwear
20. Popular swimwear brand
21. Leaves the dock
22. One of Alcott's "Little Women"
24. Agnus ___ (Lamb of God)
25. Nine-digit ID org.
26. Scrooge's expletive
29. Practice boxing
31. Session: abbr.
33. Jai ___
35. Swift, compact horse
37. Exhorts
41. Shears for a hair pro
44. Foe
45. Beer foam
46. Basic seasoning
47. Harden
49. Miffed state
51. Domicile: abbr.
52. Spot of land in the Seine
55. Opening
57. Mrs. David Copperfield
59. Tinny-sounding
62. "Give a ring sometime!"
66. Griddle utensils
68. Soft Dutch cheeses
69. Repetitive learning process
70. Does a gardening chore
71. Zaps with a stun gun
72. Lith. and Ukr., formerly
73. Assistant

DOWN

1. Eyes, poetically
2. Dickens's Uriah
3. Like many a New England "shoppe"
4. Mount in Exodus
5. Have a good day on the links
6. Prepare to fire
7. "Swiss Family Robinson" author Johann
8. Did a cobbler's job
9. Enjoys thoroughly, as praise, slangily
10. AOL and others
11. Mets' stadium's dedicatee et al.
12. Geisha's footwear
13. Inventor and electrical engineer Nikolai
18. Praise-filled poems
19. News bit
23. Severe
26. Like a ___ in the woods
27. Actor Alda
28. Loser to the tortoise
30. Track meet events
32. Orgs.
34. Some PCs
36. Not at all spicy
38. Equipment
39. ___ Stanley Gardner
40. Retired sound-breakers
42. Monocle
43. Extreme follies
48. Use a phone
50. Ensnare
52. Egg on
53. "You can ___ ___ horse to water…"
54. Old lab burners
56. Marina sights
58. First Greek letter
60. Topmost

61. Corp. money chiefs

63. First of 13 popes

64. Classic TV's talking horse

65. Caesar's existence

67. Env. content, maybe

Answers on page 172.

Breakfast's Ready

ACROSS

1. Pursue
6. Oak nut
11. Possessed
14. Surround: 2 wds.
15. Recipient
16. Lincoln
17. Breakfast item: 2 wds.
19. Me: Fr.
20. Hit in the head
21. Actor Reynolds
22. Sleepy or Doc
24. Emcee
25. Enough
26. Bewitch
30. Collie or poodle, e.g.
31. Confirm
32. Rapture
33. Recede
36. Be
37. Stir
38. Motherless calf
40. Privileges: abbr.
41. Profession
42. Low bubbling sound
43. Sat for the painter
46. Hair
47. Commotion
49. Mardi ___

50. Use
51. ___ Day (Feb. 29)
52. Accountants: abbr.
56. French title of nobility
57. Breakfast item: 2 wds.
60. Initials of a classic rock group
61. Not suitable
62. Friendship
63. ___ Francisco
64. Assessments
65. Take it easy

DOWN

1. Ice cream flavor: abbr.
2. Protagonist
3. "___ for All Seasons": 2 wds.
4. Piece of plumbing
5. Elizabeth's land: abbr.
6. Adapt
7. Tennis area
8. "Sit ___!": 2 wds.
9. Part of R & R: abbr.
10. Tool for a seamstress
11. Breakfast items: 3 wds.
12. Scrap a space project
13. Make into a god
18. Black wood
23. Tiny

24. Sword handle
25. Use a crowbar
26. Always
27. Succeeding
28. Breakfast item: 2 wds.
29. Towel designation
30. Carton
32. Triangular sail
34. Ill humor
35. Hive dwellers
37. Fashionable, '60s style
38. Union jack?
39. Alternatives
41. Magruder of Watergate
42. Chart
44. Japanese sash
45. Brimstone
46. Pamphlets
47. Hell
48. Part of the soft palate
49. Aladdin's friend
51. Not right
52. Arrive
53. Bucket
54. Dog of literature
55. Underworld river
58. Genetic material: abbr.
59. Pitch

Answers on page 172.

Let's Get Away from It All

ACROSS

1. Bio and chem, e.g.
5. British nobleman
9. Man of morals?
14. Sighed words
15. Medical picture
16. Courageous
17. Early television situation comedy: 4 wds.
20. Other than
21. Jealousy
22. Before, poetically
23. Infamous Roman emperor
25. Mt. Rushmore's state: abbr.
27. Sleep state, for short
30. Merit
32. Busybodies
36. Medical school subj.: abbr.
38. New corp. hires
40. Editor's mark
41. "Get lost!": 5 wds.
44. Dangerous bacteria
45. Scarlett's plantation
46. Skin cream additive
47. Like a high-pitched scream
49. Spinnaker, for one
51. Sunday talk: abbr.
52. Commoner
54. Shawl or stole
56. Salty expanse
59. "___ to please!": 2 wds.
61. Enchants
65. "Come on, stay a while!": 4 wds.
68. Japanese, perhaps
69. Campus club, commonly
70. Simple melody
71. Leases
72. ___ Fifth Avenue
73. Observes

DOWN

1. Mall attraction
2. General Mills cereal
3. Apple computer product
4. Lucky number, for some
5. Highway egress: 2 wds.
6. Sculpture or dance
7. $10/hour, say
8. French silk center
9. Being temporarily set aside
10. Important time period
11. Use a piggy bank
12. Above
13. Pierre's pop
18. Blunted sword
19. Some briefs, briefly
24. Planet's path
26. Australian eucalyptus eater
27. Rants and raves
28. Methuselah's father
29. Of prime importance
31. Grannies
33. Tough exams
34. Tea type
35. Beef source
37. Bloom associated with Holland
39. Barn floor covering
42. A great deal
43. Salon offerings
48. Bit of foliage
50. Cowardly Lion portrayer
53. Punches
55. Formal agreements
56. Play the lead
57. Abate
58. Similar (to)
60. Pianist Hess
62. Lecher
63. Lion's locks
64. French holy women: abbr.
66. Chow down
67. Acorn's future identity

Answers on page 172.

For the Birds

ACROSS

1. Very bitter
6. Pager summons
10. Unwanted e-mail
14. Big zoo animal
15. A, as in Edison
16. Crunchy Tex-Mex munchie
17. Mean business: 2 wds.
19. "...___ put it another way": 2 wds.
20. Poet's before
21. Means justification, to some
22. Shoveled coal into
24. Some Ivy Leaguers
25. Phrase in many church names
26. Shade of blue
29. Drink greedily: 2 wds.
30. "Shake___!": 2 wds.
31. Auction stipulation
33. Black billiard ball
37. "The ___ McCoys"
38. Kind of guitar in country music
40. Largest Mariana Island
41. Ladies' man
43. Civil Rights activist Parks
44. Fashion magazine

45. Permanent place?
47. Major event in golf: 2 wds.
49. Brit's "buddy": 2 wds.
52. Moran of "Happy Days"
53. Like a sponge
54. "Jeopardy!" host Trebek
55. Hellenic H
58. Jacob's hairy brother
59. Humbly admitting error: 2 wds.
62. Money for the landlord
63. Pro ___: Lat.
64. Name on jetliners, once
65. Synagogue chests
66. Utters
67. Bad-tempered

DOWN

1. Comedian Johnson
2. Blacken, as steak
3. Get under one's skin
4. Pen contents
5. "Go on!": 2 wds.
6. Poets on heroic themes
7. Members at lodge?
8. Night before Christmas
9. Settles a tab: 2 wds.
10. Informer: 2 wds.

11. Hooded jacket
12. Put on a show
13. Temperamental
18. Football Hall of Famer Johnny
23. T, on many exams
24. Boys with badges: 2 wds.
25. Desert refuges
26. Singer Vikki
27. Breakfast spread
28. Smile from ear to ear
29. Rest atop: 2 wds.
32. Barber's sharpener
34. Swallow eagerly
35. In good health
36. Untouchables, et al
39. Designer Ralph
42. Pearl Harbor locale
46. Printer parts
48. Oater pistol
49. "Don Giovanni," e.g.
50. Luckless one
51. Didn't pass the bar?
52. Inventor Howe
54. ABA member: abbr.
55. Significant periods
56. "Nothing ___!": 2 wds.
57. Out of kilter
60. Travel org.
61. J.E.B. Stuart's country

Answers on page 173.

Profit in Baskets

ACROSS

1. Carpenter's holder
5. Satellite receiver
9. Chew the fat
12. Publisher Adolph
13. Black and white sandwich
14. A, in Arles
15. Unconscious state: 2 wds.
17. Neither Rep. nor Dem.
18. Abduct
19. More nasty
21. T or F, on exams: abbr.
22. Playground cry
24. ___ noir
25. "The Wizard ___": 2 wds.
26. Irish poet and playwright
27. All profit, in the NBA?: 3 wds.
31. Words before "a time": 2 wds.
32. Swiss mountains
33. NY Met, for one
34. Get ready
35. No-goodnik
38. Upper house
40. Danny of "Do the Right Thing"
42. Chiang ___-shek
43. Gift from a bunny
45. Direct ending
46. Land measure
47. Sir's counterpart
48. The, in Berlin
49. Tim of "Sister, Sister"
50. It's figured in square feet

DOWN

1. Screwdriver ingredient
2. Cause winter isolation
3. Takes off
4. Armchair athlete's channel
5. Miami athlete
6. Rage
7. Terse summons: 2 wds.
8. Show optimism
9. Certain African
10. Bening of "American Beauty"
11. Treatment for many illnesses
16. Deemed appropriate
20. Helps during the heist
23. Mystery writers' award
25. Mitchell's Scarlett
26. Modern affluent type
27. Like studded tires
28. Enjoying a furlough
29. More minute
30. Sounded off, like a lamb
34. Type of sign or pipe
35. Like crystal
36. Simple plants
37. Accepted doctrine
39. Pull apart
41. Humorist Bombeck
44. Hindu title

Answers on page 173.

Wax On, Wax Off

ACROSS

1. Former transcontinental planes: abbr.
5. Snoozes
9. 21st letter of the Greek alphabet
12. Gumbo vegetable
13. Leave out
14. German article
15. Illegal corn liquor
17. Took a stool
18. Republic in southeast Africa
19. Cauldron
21. Building extension
22. And others: abbr.
24. Not as dark
25. Church structure
27. Proverbial lookalikes
28. Curry favor with
31. Let fall to the floor
32. Show again
33. Plentiful
35. Insecticide banned since 1973
36. X-ray alternative
39. Coral producers
41. Sure winner
43. Singer/actress Zadora
44. Wearing one's birthday suit
46. Show fallibility
47. "Goodbye, Sophia"
48. ___ Royale National Park
49. Object, in law
50. Pack away
51. Prophet

DOWN

1. French department or river
2. A toast to one's health
3. Wild-haired doll
4. Yemen's capital
5. Pitcher's dream game
6. French friend
7. Variety of champagne
8. Exorbitant, for a price
9. Grinding tools
10. Florida racetrack
11. Buries
16. Just peachy
20. Mammal with a long snout
23. Like a bullfighter
25. Make use of
26. "Antiques ___"
28. Movable cupboard
29. Columnar trees
30. Flexible
31. Well-dressed
34. Many Biblical films
36. Clock climber, in a nursery rhyme
37. Shoulder firearm
38. Suggest
40. State of irritation
42. Japanese sashes
45. Universal ideal

Answers on page 173.

A Matter of Time

ACROSS

1. Ralph of "The Waltons"
6. Chef's meas.
9. Dunderhead
12. Incorporate, as into a city
13. DDT-banning org.
14. Health-care grp.
15. Word after rubber or food
16. Giving more lip
18. Kind of timing
20. Suppresses: 2 wds.
22. Cow's comment
23. Alliance formed in 1860: abbr.
24. Freezing cold
26. Wander
30. Current
34. Color changer
35. Took the gold medal
36. Some plasma screens
37. Gas price-watching org.
40. Beat badly
42. Noon
46. Google is a major one
47. Presses
50. ___ whim: 2 wds.
51. Unprocessed
52. Fry in a pan
53. Muddy home
54. Ambulance destinations (abbr.)
55. Vote in, as a president

DOWN

1. "Able ___ I ere I..."
2. Uninvited picnic guest
3. On pins and needles: 3 wds.
4. Part-time workers
5. Heroic act
6. It may require writing an essay
7. Uncontrollable muscle action
8. A slow stroll, perhaps in Spain
9. Where Dayton is
10. Interjection of agreement
11. Edsel maker
17. Treat with contempt
19. One-twelfth of a foot
20. Iraqi missile
21. "___ with my little eye...": 2 wds.
25. Archery bow wood
27. Win a debate
28. Rugged roadsters (abbr.)
29. Netting
31. Doctorate hurdle
32. Nighttime flier
33. Not farmed out
38. Burning up
39. Rosy perfume
41. Living on a farm, perhaps
42. The terrible ___
43. Left
44. Cyberspace auction site
45. Conforms strictly
48. Truncation abbreviation
49. Arranged

Answers on page 173.

Patriotic Songs

ACROSS

1. Emotional shock
5. Stare at the stars
9. Mr. T's squad, with "The"
14. Kind of rug
15. Most populous continent
16. Creator of Winnie the Pooh
17. 1995 hit song by TLC
20. Enjoys a bath
21. Two times five
22. Came closer to
26. Fully gratify a desire
30. Holiday song crooned by Crosby
34. "The Man Who Mistook His Wife for ___ ___"
35. Boxer Spinks who beat Ali
36. Skins an apple
37. Sprees
39. Last name of Stallone's Rocky
40. An inert gas
41. Rocky for Stallone
44. A lot of
45. Footwear in an Elvis Presley song
48. Nile snakes
49. Must
50. One ___ ___ time
51. Sheriff's star
56. What the answers to 17-, 30-, and 45-Across contain
63. Harvests
64. Ark builder
65. Sigh word
66. With 32-Down, newswoman Linda Ellerbee's tag line
67. Japanese wrestling
68. Title fish in a 2003 animated movie

DOWN

1. Containers
2. Three-layer cookie
3. She dallied with a swan
4. Speak
5. Practical joke
6. ___ Wednesday
7. Pimple
8. Defunct airline
9. Prayer ending
10. First X or O in a 3-in-a-row game
11. Yale student
12. Santa ___ winds
13. Actor/director Gibson
18. Ain't right?
19. Prefix for cure or cab
23. Shocking fish
24. Top card
25. Greek letter before sigma
26. Patron saint of sailors
27. One-celled organisms
28. Eagle's claws
29. Test that's not true/false
30. Spins
31. End a phone call
32. See 66-Across
33. Health resort
34. Addis ___ (capital of Ethiopia)
38. Naval rank: Abbr.
39. Tops
41. Once again gains money or trust
42. Poem of praise
43. Was ahead
46. "For ___ us a child is born..."
47. Traveling tramp
50. In addition
52. Actor Alda
53. Loser to Clinton
54. Unit of mass
55. Old gas brand

56. "… ___ ___ mouse?"
57. Famed KC QB Dawson
58. Mom's spouse
59. In-car location finder
60. With 56-Down, "Are ___ a man…"
61. America's uncle
62. Korean American comic Margaret

Answers on page 174.

Echoes

ACROSS

1. Banana cover
5. Off-base illegally
9. Pecs' neighbors
12. BBs and bullets, e.g.
13. Skirt length
14. Brazilian vacation destination, for short
15. 1980s detective TV series
18. Copy editor's bane
19. Lord's mate
20. Menacing
23. Cooking amt.
26. Flimflam
29. Biblical woman
30. Hooded winter jacket
31. Repeatedly
34. Flash of light
35. Late columnist Landers
36. Explosive letters
37. Hand-in-the-door reaction
38. Tiananmen Square, for one
40. Toothed wheel
42. Scat singer Fitzgerald
45. In circles
50. Solo in "Star Wars"
51. Not natural, for hair
52. "Render therefore ___ Caesar..."
53. Nods, perhaps
54. JFK sights
55. Lecturer's platform

DOWN

1. Mas' mates
2. Send out, as energy
3. TV award
4. Belt holders
5. Dr.'s org.
6. Be victorious
7. How eccentrics behave
8. Bart Simpson's sibling
9. Base boy, perhaps
10. Book jacket blurb, often
11. Bart, to Homer
16. Harmful
17. Name holder at a convention
21. An ex of Artie
22. Of the kidneys
24. Scrape, as a knee
25. Show windedness
26. Clever
27. Come-hither look
28. Carpentry tools
30. WWII tank
32. Done permanently, as writing
33. Modern-day evidence
38. Supplicates
39. How storybooks are often read
41. Includes
43. Colorful moth
44. "Nay!" sayer
45. Letter used as a density symbol
46. Sturdy tree
47. Tennis court divider
48. Orthodontist's deg.
49. Shindigs

Answers on page 174.

Explore Your Mind

ACROSS

1. Oil market cartel: abbr.
5. Maker of pens and lighters
8. Use an ax
12. Part of the foot
13. The end of an ___
14. Pushy and unfriendly
15. Leader of the first circumnavigation of the world
17. Prophetic sign
18. Feel poorly
19. Pull on a chain
21. First Spaniard to reach Florida
26. Minor slip
27. "___ River Valley"
28. Temporary bed
30. "Let Us Now Praise Famous Men" writer James
31. Swindle
32. Simple, flowerless plant
33. Part of MPH
34. To's opposite
35. Salute with wine
36. He blazed the Wilderness Road into Kentucky
39. Popular hedging plant
40. Direction on a submarine
41. Economic gain
44. Leader of four expeditions to the New World
49. Old West lawman Wyatt
50. WWW address
51. Basic currency of Italy since 1999
52. Bridge shape
53. Some NFL linemen: abbr.
54. Location of zip code 10001: abbr.

DOWN

1. Unit of electrical resistance
2. Toy shooter's ammo
3. Brain scan: abbr.
4. Remove stains from
5. Heroine of Disney's "Beauty and the Beast"
6. "Rosemary's Baby" author Levin
7. Military snack bar
8. Oscar winner Russell
9. Drone
10. Poem of praise
11. Write
16. Biting insects
20. Advanced in age
21. Flipped through a book
22. Coloratura's genre
23. Slobber
24. View from the coast
25. Like the Vikings
26. Once around the track
29. High explosive
31. Short hairdo
32. They accompanied Cinderella to the ball
34. Expression of disapproval
35. Vegetarian's protein source
37. Beautiful maiden
38. Snooker targets
41. "Petticoat Junction" star Benaderet
42. Sculling need
43. Tolkien creature
45. Mine output
46. Purchase
47. Coffee dispenser
48. ___ sauce

Answers on page 174.

Autumn Delight

ACROSS

1. Rainy day infield cover
5. Part of Batman's getup
9. Jazz musician ___ Calloway
12. Margarine
13. Patron saint of Norway
14. Apple pie ___ mode
15. Natural downside of Autumn
18. "Born in the ___," Bruce Springsteen song
19. Lipton product
20. Sibling's daughter
21. Prepare a salad, perhaps
23. Madam's counterpart
24. Sad news item, briefly
26. Forever, seemingly
27. Health club feature
30. Autumn sporting events
34. Ardent devotee
35. Sort
36. Salsa and French onion, e.g.
37. High or low card
38. Crucifix
40. Like a dishonest deal
43. "Hey, that hurt!"
44. Acquired
47. In autumn, students look forward to this... or do they?
50. Lyricist Gershwin
51. Fireplace fodder
52. Data, informally
53. Snoop around
54. Shorten a sentence, maybe
55. "Hey buddy... over here!"

DOWN

1. Vegetarian staple
2. "Sad to say..."
3. Kinship
4. Vote seeker, briefly
5. Ice cream holders
6. Pond scum
7. Chum
8. Time for a soiree
9. Hangout for bats
10. Actor Guinness
11. Pedestal
16. "___ a girl!"
17. Ventilate
22. Giant Mel of Cooperstown
23. Our sun
24. "Keep ___ the Grass"
25. Feathery scarf
26. BPOE member
27. Tiny amounts
28. Vim
29. Beast of burden
31. Eco-friendly transport
32. Ginger ___ (soft drink)
33. Botheration
37. Commercials
38. Perch
39. Barn bird
40. Little cut
41. Munich Mister
42. Not home
43. Bear or Berra
45. Dimwits
46. Horse's gait
48. Brick carrier
49. Puppy sound

Answers on page 174.

Fit to Be Tied

ACROSS
1. Expression of wonderment
4. Approval of a comic
8. Atty. General's cabinet division
11. "The Jungle Book" snake
12. Combination of protons, neutrons, and electrons
13. Look amazed
14. Play double Dutch
16. John Steinbeck's "East of ___"
17. Raconteur's stock-in-trade
19. Diaper, in Soho
21. Evaluate, as ore
22. End of Jack Horner's boast
23. Two-faced
26. Face impending danger
32. Young dragonfly
33. Tiny drink
34. Up till now
37. Agronomists' study
39. Often on the bench
43. Banjoist Scruggs
44. Not practical
47. Antelopes, to lions
48. Deft
49. Stylistically imitative of
50. Long-faced
51. Tournament passes
52. Azure expanse

DOWN
1. Agrees to
2. Sturdy furniture material
3. Kind of sharp turn
4. Flying predator of Greek myth
5. High on
6. Snake dancers
7. Act of Contrition finale
8. Tots' pops
9. "Tosca," e.g.
10. "___ from the Block," Lopez song
13. Spewing hot spring
15. Chirp
18. Wound deeply
19. "No dice"
20. Org. for doctors
23. Casual memo letters
24. Driver's org.
25. British Inc.
27. Like an old tree trunk
28. Tribal minstrel
29. Inexplicable occurrences
30. Feel poorly
31. Infield coups: abbr.
34. Ways up
35. Family name in "Gone With the Wind"
36. Put in a kiln
37. Slaw, fries, etc.
38. Single
40. Swedish auto
41. Frozen dessert chain
42. Smoker's sound
45. Similar type
46. Small island

Answers on page 175.

Help by Another Name

ACROSS

1. Fake hair
4. Practice boxing
8. Snoozes
12. Fifth in NYC, e.g.
13. Spanish bull
14. "That's interesting"
15. Deli sandwich choice
17. When clock hands form a right angle
18. It's a two-by-four, Mr. Nicholson
20. Make a movie
23. Fruit of the Loom competitor
24. "As I see it," in chat room shorthand
25. Triathlete's need
28. It's a TV ad, Mr. Linkletter
34. City of northern France
35. Imitator
36. Swamped
40. Broadway dancer
41. He's a physician, Mr. Clinton
45. Prefix with focus
46. X, in calculus
50. Forest opening
51. One of "The Waltons"
52. Paddle
53. Small whirlpool
54. Score silence
55. Log splitter

DOWN

1. Opposite of peace
2. League plant?
3. Expression of mild surprise
4. Cocky walk
5. Where feet are divisions of a meter
6. Spirited horse
7. Went by horse, say
8. Silent Japanese assassin
9. Afghan or Thai
10. Coins of old Cambridge
11. Tries to locate
16. Burgeon
19. "Cheers" costar Perlman
20. Attack dog command
21. Med. insurance plan
22. Electrical resistance unit
25. Unseen means of support
26. Sprain reliever
27. Uncles and aunts
29. Comeback, of sorts
30. 1972 Derek and the Dominos hit
31. Killer ___
32. High-___ monitor
33. Endeavor
36. Bit of folk wisdom
37. Part of WWJD?
38. Played charades
39. Coldhearted
40. Sparkle
42. Vacationer in a camper, informally
43. Like Old Mother Hubbard's cupboard
44. Part of the uvea
47. Squeezing reptile
48. Not strict
49. Before, of yore

Answers on page 175.

It's Magic

ACROSS

1. "Show Boat" character ___ Andy
5. Cash outlet, for short
8. Kindergarten terror
12. Ball-shape hairdo
13. "La la" preceder
14. Country singer and sitcom star McEntire
15. Cheer (for)
16. Discuss
18. Passion inducer, of a sort
20. Drink too much
21. Genre for "The Outer Limits"
25. Eagle's roost
29. Razz
30. Amulet
35. Torah holder
36. Farmer's refrain?
37. Out of bed
40. Off-road buggies
43. Recipient of stickpins
48. Icy area to the north or south
51. "And if ___ before..."
52. Slangy British pounds
53. Battleship score
54. Present unfairly
55. Vex
56. 1940s spy org.
57. Not soft

DOWN

1. Director Reiner
2. Under way
3. Brigham Young University city
4. Steno's book
5. On the subject of
6. Not this
7. Landlocked North African nation
8. Rodeo horse
9. Religious title: abbr.
10. "Barney Miller" actor Vigoda
11. Roofing substance
17. Drops to the floor, in the ring
19. Shed sunburned skin
22. CPA's recommendation, perhaps
23. Tree with lights, often
24. Company based in Armonk, NY
26. Have regrets
27. Here, to Pierre
28. Squeeze (out)
30. Long-nosed fish
31. "Either it goes ___ do"
32. Permits
33. "Adios"
34. Pot luck contribution
38. Get around
39. "Neither a borrower ___..."
41. Bloody Mary ingredient
42. Less direct
44. Jorge's eight
45. Rostrum
46. Stops vacillating
47. Beyond suggestive
48. NO followers
49. Equivalent of "ja"
50. "___ ol' me?"

Answers on page 175.

Use Some Sense

ACROSS

1. Continuous movement
5. Dog that spotted Peter Pan
9. Revival technique
12. "No sweat"
13. Run amok
14. Arles assent
15. Be suspicious
17. Orderly supervisors: abbr.
18. Shopaholic's activity
19. Court shout
21. Do some work on a dairy farm
24. Kind of test
25. Mischievous sort
28. Without restraint
32. Sport without tackling
35. 1982 NCAA basketball champs
36. The heavens
37. Corn spike
38. Hard-to-break hold
41. Become furious
44. Otherworldly
48. Dernier ___ (latest thing)
49. Food sampling
52. Coffee container
53. "Aha!"
54. Chieftain's charge
55. Chinese restaurant syndrome substance
56. Chew the fat
57. Georgetown athlete

DOWN

1. Parker who played Crockett
2. Light fixture
3. Computer customer
4. Tree tissue
5. Pistol-packing PAC
6. Ventilate
7. Dad on the ark
8. Stab, of sorts
9. Bullfight arenas
10. Shrimpish
11. Court order?
16. Floral neckpiece
20. Sheik's subject
22. Longest prison sentence
23. Hillock
25. Cousin on "The Addams Family"
26. Extinct flightless bird
27. Turning to mush
29. Not great
30. Certain lodge member
31. Stallone nickname
33. Cook too hot
34. Religious dissenter
39. Bee follower
40. Two-master
41. Riffraff
42. Miscalculates
43. Fast race
45. Move, in real estate lingo
46. Holmesian exclamation
47. Active European volcano
50. Dead ___ Scrolls
51. Vietnamese celebration

Answers on page 175.

'70s Fads

ACROSS

1. Computer available in "Bondi blue"
5. RN's skill
8. Tax helpers, for short
12. Dr. Zhivago's love
13. Tow truck summoner
14. Waikiki's island
15. Big test
16. Driven
18. 1970s fad
20. Luftwaffe opposer in WWII
21. Appear
22. 1970s fad
26. Levitate
29. Sailor's affirmative
30. Nighttime noise
33. Nothing
34. City or sight in Arizona
36. 1970s fad
38. Rose banned from baseball
41. "Make ___ double"
42. 1970s fad
46. Tumblers
47. Prepare for a rainy day
50. Make ready
51. Insignificant amount
52. It sells a lot of build-it-yourself furniture
53. Firecrackers with no crack
54. Opp. of WSW
55. Cry in the doctor's office

DOWN

1. Suffix with percent
2. Factor in the makeup business
3. Riyadh resident
4. Minolta product
5. Rear end feature on a 1950s car
6. Sheep's youngster
7. Mob bosses
8. "I'm Not Lisa" singer Jessi
9. Golden horse
10. "Excuse me!"
11. Dishwasher's sinkful
17. Summer in France
19. Young men
22. Machine part
23. Seeded player's privilege
24. Breathed in and out
25. "Alley ___" (comic strip)
27. [Their mistake, not mine]
28. Large American deer
31. Print anew
32. Caesar's final reproach
35. ___ Fables
37. Dried grape
39. Place for a bath
40. Delete
42. "Dragnet" force, in brief
43. Stockings shade
44. Jacket style named after a school
45. Grab
48. Annoy
49. Have lunch

Answers on page 176.

Records

ACROSS

1. Estuaries
5. Brain waves
10. Absent
14. Seven-year problem
15. Goof
16. Miss: Sp. abbr.
17. Record: 3 wds.
19. Window part
20. Helix-wise
21. Precisely: 3 wds.
23. Baseball's Otis
24. To perfume
25. Described vividly
28. Fondler
31. Poem type
32. Paste-on
34. Move crab-wise
35. VIP's wheels, for short
37. Is intrepid
39. ___ me tangere: Lat.
40. Aerobatic thrills
42. Skewered morsel: sp. var.
44. Victory
45. Flowed past
47. Marsh birds
49. Pavlova and Magnani
50. Overstuff
51. Criticized
53. Shook
57. Took the bus
58. Records: 3 wds.
60. Burden
61. Leaning
62. Beach sight
63. Certain voters: abbr.
64. Mean
65. Featured one

DOWN

1. Tears
2. "Run ___ the flagpole...": 2 wds.
3. Play start: 2 wds.
4. WWII navigating system
5. Blew inward
6. Tunes in
7. Catch sight of
8. Fruit punch
9. Mail machine
10. Type of bug
11. Records: 2 wds.
12. Tamarisk
13. Ivy League campus
18. Cleped
22. Individuals
24. Biblical spy
25. Lounges
26. Mooncalf
27. Written record
28. Concerned
29. Little Eleanor
30. Wagon controls
33. Dessert choices
36. Candor
38. Church area
41. Reasoned
43. Cheer for the diva
46. Lunatic
48. Puts right
50. Thorax
51. Poke
52. Tops: hyph.
53. Schusses
54. Easy win
55. View from Taormina
56. Forest creature
59. ___ mode: 2 wds.

Answers on page 176.

Crossing Caution

ACROSS

1. Bovine baby
5. Shankar of sitar
9. Synagogue official
14. Cain's brother
15. Seuss's "If __ __ the Zoo"
16. Kept in the dark
17. Fish in a melt
18. Unsteady gait
19. City near Florence
20. Breaking news order
23. Protrudes
24. Vine-covered
25. Sporty Chevy
28. Sneaker brand
29. New Deal prog.
32. Big name in gas
33. Furnace output
34. Restaurateur Toots
35. "You're one to spout off!"
38. Lodging providers
39. Skin moisturizer
40. Perform better than
41. NFL 3-pointers
42. Type of school
43. Annoy forcefully
44. Caribbean republic
46. Challenging chore
47. "Think it over"
52. Titanic-seeker's tool
53. Cry of frustration
54. Boat follower
55. Office worker
56. Cold war defense assn.
57. Former blade brand
58. Soda insert
59. Kind of jacket
60. Wine list datum

DOWN

1. Rodent exterminators
2. Share a border
3. Jay of TV
4. Pancakes
5. "Sure thing!"
6. Ovine sign
7. Theda Bara role
8. Behind closed doors
9. Putin's land
10. Liqueur flavoring
11. Use all the resources of
12. Waste containers
13. "Give ___ ___ rest"
21. Novelist Scott
22. Madonna musical
25. Ariz. neighbor
26. In the midst of
27. White lightning maker
28. Noted fabulist
30. Polliwogs' places
31. Job-specific vocabulary
33. Golfer's dream
34. Leave stealthily
36. Author Bret
37. At large
42. NASCAR service area
43. Strand on an island
45. Yoga posture
46. Jay Silverheels role
47. Senator Trent
48. What this isn't
49. Glut
50. Gumbo vegetable
51. Get closer to
52. Draft letters

Answers on page 176.

Hurry!

ACROSS

1. Wild guess
5. Mont Blanc, for example
8. Did in
12. Columbus's home
13. Civil War general
14. Scruff
15. "Hurry!"
17. Like
18. One for the books?
19. Facet
21. Frittata
23. Circumspect
27. Small Pacific salmons
31. Aptly named fruit
32. Slow-witted
34. Presidential caucus state
35. Dark-meat choice
37. Bread crumbs, perhaps
39. Like last-minute chores, often
41. Small bar
44. Kind of report
49. First place?
50. "Hurry!"
52. Matador's opponent
53. Sensitive subject, to some
54. Writer Ferber
55. Side order
56. Heir, perhaps
57. 49-across inhabitant

DOWN

1. Counter order
2. Friends' pronoun
3. Isn't incorrect?
4. Two out of two
5. Worried, and then some
6. Maui memento
7. Corolla part
8. "Hurry!"
9. Superior, for one
10. Like a DeMille production
11. Left
16. Club choice
20. Dry, as champagne
22. Ruler's decree
23. Kind of instinct
24. "That's disgusting"
25. Baba of "Arabian Nights"
26. "Hurry!"
28. ___ polloi
29. Fess (up)
30. Droop
33. Wet a little
36. Part of HMS
38. Book after John
40. Counter orders
41. Wagers
42. Superstar
43. Immunizing stuff
45. Word with code or rug
46. Mary Lincoln, née ___
47. Arm bone
48. Bridge coup
51. Pride

Answers on page 176.

"Easy" Does It

ACROSS

1. "I'm glad that's over!"
5. Edit from the tape
10. Nongentile
13. Mae West's invite, in part: 2 wds.
14. Superman star
15. Baaed girl
16. Circe and Lorelei
18. Shirt kind
19. Incessantly
20. Excited, with "up"
21. Insignificant sort
23. Misplayed at bridge
25. Worthless?
27. Bishopric
28. Unmatched
32. French seaport
35. 14-Across's role
36. "Death and Fire" artist
37. Potent wriggler
38. Lady Di's family name
41. Mrs.: Fr., abbr.
42. "Holy cow!"
44. Oceanbound flier
45. A.k.a. Barnaby Jones
47. Unexpected successes
49. Spelldown
50. Oculist's creation
51. Establishes
55. Pup
58. Game, ___, match
59. SOS
60. "A mouse!"
61. Legendary ballplayer: 3 wds.
65. Churchillean gesture
66. Completed
67. Fouled up
68. Chicago trains, for short
69. Rushes
70. Admit, with "up"

DOWN

1. Annoy
2. Muscle Beach denizens: hyph.
3. Josephine, e.g.
4. Soppy
5. Poodle or Peke
6. "___ we forget"
7. Undergoers of: suf.
8. Garden gal
9. See 1-Down
10. "___ plumerai": Fr., 2 wds.
11. Pitcher
12. Turn on the waterworks
13. Gag or gang ending
17. Name in Korea's history
22. Bubbly bandmaster
24. Understands
25. Mugwump's perch
26. Network
28. William's kin
29. O'Neill's "Desire" site
30. Dotted, coat-of-arms-wise
31. Spotted
32. Entreats
33. Tackle-box item
34. Robert ___: 2 wds.
35. Jean and Deborah
39. Hammerhead part
40. "___ pleat," zoot suit feature
43. Former governor and senator Miller
46. Show up: 2 wds.
48. Mill contents
49. ___ noire
51. Burpee's wares
52. Lascivious looks
53. "It's nobody ___ business"
54. Drove 80
55. "___ Only Just Begun"
56. Scoundrel
57. Barely makes it
58. Garbo's home: abbr.
62. Compass point
63. Town near Arhem
64. Zebra on the field, for short

Answers on page 177.

Summertime Fun

ACROSS

1. Give up, as a territory
5. Nautical assent
8. Scottish girl
12. Get-out-of-jail cash
13. Drink like a kitten
14. Director Kazan
15. Summertime warmer
17. Waiter's handout
18. "Gosh!"
19. "On the Road" writer Jack
21. Restaurant bill, informally
23. Wish undone
25. Loosen, as a shoelace
26. Pole or Czech
28. Vintage photograph shade
30. Flower features
32. Make beloved
36. Kitchen gadget
38. Major show, briefly
39. Capital of Jordan
42. It precedes Sept.
44. Teacher's favorite
45. Knitted baby shoes
47. Major ISP
49. Play opener: 2 wds.
50. Summertime destination
54. "Scat!"
55. Priest's robe
56. By mouth
57. Merit
58. Put into service
59. Egg layers

DOWN

1. Cronkite's former employer
2. ___ de Cologne
3. Nutcase
4. "What ___ is new?"
5. "The Greatest" prizefighter
6. Northern Civil War soldier
7. Sporting blade
8. Summertime quaff
9. Native Alaskan
10. Mount in Exodus
11. Spaghetti topper
16. That girl
20. Wreck
21. Cookbook meas.
22. Pub offering
24. Cold War letters
27. Summertime respite from school
29. Lima's land
31. Unaccompanied
33. Emulate Christopher Columbus
34. Imitate
35. Deteriorate
37. Portrait painters' stands
39. Humiliate
40. Cocoa-flavored coffee
41. Car engine
43. Car fuel
46. Jacob's twin
48. "Yikes!": hyph.
51. Lincoln's nickname
52. Hightailed it
53. Golf legend Ernie

Answers on page 177.

Dairy Folk

ACROSS

1. Audi competitor
4. In a crowd of
8. Juicy fruit
12. Item worn around the neck
13. Baked southern dish
14. Tops
15. Sushi bar staple
17. Cause to wince
18. Timid folk
20. Intoxicate
23. Snap course
24. One of Shakespeare's villains
25. Inspiration source
28. Clumsy folk
34. "Love Makes the World Go Round" singer Jackson
35. Brigham Young's home
36. Dwight's opponent in '52 and '56
40. Acting profession
41. Ineffectual folk
45. Temple's first husband
46. Where grapes grow
50. Wrestling style
51. One of the Great Lakes
52. F or G, but not H
53. Straddle
54. "___ Blue"
55. Feller in the woods

DOWN

1. Hardly the big shot
2. Dairy sound
3. The Appian ___
4. Distinguished (from)
5. Pained expression
6. Ancient Machu Picchu dweller
7. Consider
8. ___ New Guinea
9. Goofs off
10. Make whole
11. The brainy bunch
16. Run quickly
19. Hammer feature
20. Lobster-eater's attire
21. It's found dans le bain
22. "___ Bilko," Steve Martin film
25. Soldier's fare, for short
26. Mystery flyer
27. Pride, lust, or envy
29. Amend text
30. Full of determination
31. Terminal posting: abbr.
32. Kind of doll
33. The queen as a subject?
36. Hoard
37. Root out
38. Long-necked animal
39. Ohio's "City of Invention"
40. Trusty mount
42. Dutch ___
43. Gossamer
44. Take a short cut?
47. Rap sheet letters
48. Carnivorous dinosaur name
49. Hair colorer

Answers on page 177.

Venomous

ACROSS

1. Messy eater's protection
4. Diet soda from Coca-Cola
7. Movie western
12. Bruce Springsteen's "Born in the ___"
13. In the manner of
14. Temperature taker
15. PC link, for short
16. Invertebrate with stinging tentacles
18. ___ California
20. GameCube alternative
21. Formation of flying geese
22. Arthropod with a stinging tail
24. Actress Lollebrigida
25. Parks in front of bus?
26. Religious pamphlet
27. Madras garments
30. Backless slippers
31. Show without a doubt
32. Check the price of, in a way
34. Provide relief
35. Swimmer with a barbed tail
39. Court grp.
40. Head for the heights
41. Roof projection
42. Longest venomous snake
45. Restriction
46. "Delta Dawn" singer Tucker
47. Blockhead
48. Small amount
49. Lunchtime, for some
50. Jargon suffix
51. In poor health

DOWN

1. Light sources
2. Asimov of science fiction
3. Picked instrument
4. ___ Mahal
5. Joan's role on "Dynasty"
6. Surname of fictional boxer
7. Cameo stone
8. "___ Wiedersehen"
9. Kind of pursuit?
10. Spirit
11. Puts in a microwave, maybe
17. Chaney of horror films
19. Hit the big time
23. Yoga posture
24. Rock genre out of Seattle
26. Secret Service agent, briefly
27. Have a conversation with
28. Graceful horse
29. Country singer Cash
32. Not volatile
33. Thin, wispy cloud type
35. Great Lakes' ___ Canal
36. Hassidic leader
37. Be of use
38. Barbra Streisand film
40. Fraudulent action
43. Swindle
44. Generation

Answers on page 177.

Bad Weather

ACROSS

1. Put into play
4. "___ Blue," TV show
8. What a pumpkin grows on
12. Wrinkly dog
13. Honolulu's island
14. Wrinkle remover
15. San Diego Chargers logo
18. Go after
19. Golfer Els
20. Drilling site?
21. Ore tester
23. Hosp. trauma units
24. "___ to Avoid," 1965 Herman's Hermits hit
25. Weather protection at the entrance
29. Tiny amounts
30. Occult ability
33. Female grouse
36. Ipso ___
38. Actor Davis
39. Suit maker
40. Suddenly astonished
43. "When you get right down ___ ..."
44. Beef or pork
45. Location of UFO sightings
46. Sgt. Snorkel's dog
47. Nimble
48. Road twist

DOWN

1. Missing one's bedtime
2. One seeking a mate
3. Picnic contest
4. Tally mark
5. Pull quickly
6. Fraternity letter
7. Pester for payment
8. Violinist's asset
9. Subtle sarcasm
10. "It's the truth!"
11. Participate in
16. Cap
17. Painting surface
21. Jordan's capital
22. Brewskis
24. Comedian Johnson
26. Connect with
27. Partner of aahed
28. Howard Hughes became one
31. Parts of a mutual fund
32. 1982 comedy about high schoolers
33. ___ voce
34. ___ in the dark
35. Astronaut's attire: hyph.
36. Silent film comedian Arbuckle
37. Tire filler
39. Ruler mixed up in arts?
41. In typography-speak, more than one long dash
42. Account exec.

Answers on page 178.

Get a Move On

ACROSS

1. Drinking spree
5. Repeat
9. Automobile type
14. Overhang
15. Pal
16. Grassy plain
17. Sonny's ex
18. Part
19. Lubricated
20. Way of life, in the army: 4 wds.
23. Automobile
24. Bread soaked in liquid
25. Fit ___ fiddle: 2 wds.
27. Ancient Greek promenade
31. Fight against
36. WWII battle sight: 2 wds.
38. Killer whale
40. NH city
41. Children's game: 3 wds.
44. "...partridge in ___ tree": 2 wds.
45. Withered
46. "___ the night before..."
47. Minnow
49. Drunkards
51. "You ___ There," hosted by Cronkite
52. Sticky substance
54. Showery month: abbr.
56. Old-fashioned: 3 wds.
64. City in upstate New York
65. Periods
66. Roman fiddler
67. River mouth
68. Pinball slip up
69. Cafeteria item
70. Ford flop
71. Only
72. Nick Charles's dog

DOWN

1. Georgia or Cal
2. Hawaiian isle
3. Outbid, in bridge
4. ___ firma
5. Yellowish brown
6. Sever
7. Hawaiian dance
8. Portents
9. Laggard
10. Lamb pen name
11. Spanish surrealist
12. Dill herb
13. Realm of dreams
21. Units of time: abbr.
22. One of the dwarfs
25. "___ as I'm concerned": 2 wds.
26. Excavate in layers
28. Pull
29. Table scraps
30. Pains
32. Dinner item
33. Flannel sheets, maybe: 2 wds.
34. Close at hand
35. Succinct
37. Norse king
39. Sol or space beginning
42. Initial
43. Permit
48. Negative prefix
50. College entrance exam: abbr.
53. U.S. playwright
55. Nina companion
56. Drained
57. Conger and moray
58. Despise
59. Threesome
60. Town ___ meeting
61. This: Sp.
62. Part of Q.E.D.: Lat.
63. Substitute for 32-Down
64. Lyric poem

Answers on page 178.

Pitching Records

ACROSS

1. "2001: A Space Odyssey" computer
4. Poisonous substance
9. Boxer's target
12. Yes, in Paris
13. Like a good guard
14. Freud focus
15. Pitcher with most consecutive scoreless innings (59)
18. Cowboy competitions
19. Cowboy's bed
20. Crawled out of bed
21. Reluctantly abstains from
24. Go off course
25. "Forget it!"
26. Pitcher with most career no-hitters (7)
30. Dress to the ___
31. List maker's space saver
34. Stooge
37. Language of Sri Lanka
39. Theatrical award
40. League of Nations home
41. Pitcher with most career shutouts (110)
45. Summer in Le Havre
46. Vacate
47. Type
48. Like a boiled lobster
49. Specialty
50. Maggie, to Lisa, briefly

DOWN

1. "Yippee!"
2. Roman goddess of dawn
3. Command to a dog
4. Nevada resort
5. Spanish cheers
6. Gen-___ (baby boomer's successor)
7. Kind of agent
8. Number in a series
9. He was affiliated with Peter, Paul, and Mary
10. Broker
11. Does the trick
16. Band leader Brown
17. Spanish vacation island
21. Continue a subscription
22. Makes a mistake
23. Dirty digs
25. Grandma's nickname
27. Start
28. Sass
29. Mortal enemy
32. Copenhagen's ___ Gardens
33. Chain sounds
34. Cringe
35. Diminish
36. Like a bathroom floor
37. Snicker
38. Abby's sister
40. Poli-sci subj.
42. Reindeer feeder?
43. Old car
44. Pickle container

Answers on page 178.

Horsing Around

ACROSS

1. Cambodian's neighbor
5. Communist island
9. Lotus programs co.
12. ___ sod
13. Mimicked
14. Miss Piggy's pronoun
15. Taken the place of
17. It has a small head
18. Forget a horse?
20. Radiation protection no.
21. Some batters: abbr.
22. Trumpet location
25. In a state of joy
30. Way to a dark horse?
33. Not type A
34. Former White House resident's inits.
35. Bumbling bloke
36. PD notice
39. Lighter version of the iron horse?
45. To write quickly
46. Gingham dog fighter
48. Hail
49. Coast-to-coast highway
50. Not a one
51. Color of Santa's suit
52. Fashion designer Cassini
53. They, in Italian

DOWN

1. Keep the rhythm, perhaps
2. Chuck
3. Ship's safe side
4. Innovation beginnings
5. 1962 movie thriller remade in 1991
6. Doing
7. "Where have you ___?"
8. Increased
9. Identity thief
10. One way to cook cabbage
11. Tea flavorer
16. Winner of the Hart Trophy in the NHL
19. Arctic fish
22. List-ending abbr.
23. Melodramatic cry
24. Sent in another direction
26. B followers
27. Pretty mad
28. Descartes' conclusion
29. Nancy Grace's employer
31. Paper quantity
32. Ex ___ (by virtue of position)
37. Army rank: abbr.
38. Hard stuff
39. Between open and closed
40. Nothing, in a set
41. Abbr. in many U.S. org. names
42. 1997 Peter Fonda title role
43. Key cards in 21
44. "___ and the Real Girl" (2007 movie)
47. Head opposite

Answers on page 178.

Deli Misadventures

ACROSS

1. Greek letter
4. Raised eyebrow shape
8. "Look what I did!": hyph.
12. "You've Got Mail" co.
13. Hide a treasure, maybe
14. All over again
15. "Were you puzzled over what to buy at the deli?": 5 wds.
18. Clear the windshield
19. Like a docked yacht
20. Sheepish remark?
22. Schuss
23. Somebody special
26. Martinique, par exemple
28. Like a wildly colored tie
32. "How would you describe the deli's decor?": 2 wds.
36. Menial worker
37. Pitcher's stat.
38. British explorer John
39. Participate in an auction
42. Fashion monogram
44. Nudged rudely
48. Chars
52. "And the proprietor? What was he like?": 3 wds.
54. Gait at the track
55. Skin lotion ingredient
56. Beachgoer's quest, often
57. Darns socks, maybe
58. Clucks disapprovingly
59. Wrath

DOWN

1. Bookie's worry
2. Sewing machine inventor Elias
3. Norwegian saint and king
4. First name of the second first lady
5. Stocking annoyance
6. Grouch
7. Publicizes, slangily
8. Perceptible to touch
9. Cross with a loop
10. Remove from text
11. Bowled over
16. Weep out loud
17. Vex
21. Everything
23. Big mouth
24. Have bills to pay
25. Tabloid subj.
27. Give the once-over
29. Anthem contraction
30. Red, white, and blue letters
31. Turn red, perhaps
33. Opens, as a barn door
34. Weep
35. Big bothers
40. ___ Jima
41. Skim, as milk
43. Name of 13 popes
44. Young newts
45. Tackle box item
46. Totally botch
47. Bb. 2-baggers
49. Not pro
50. Paddler's target
51. Word in a New Year's Eve song
53. "All systems go" to NASA

Have Some Moore

ACROSS

1. "___ Miniver"
4. Betelgeuse, for one
8. Commands respect from
12. Presidential nickname
13. Spiral-horned grazer
14. Coin featuring the likeness of 12-Across
15. Roger Moore's debut as James Bond
18. "Good Rockin' Daddy" singer James
19. Greg of "My Two Dads"
20. Cut finely
22. Poetic tribute
23. Earth Day prefix
24. Chamber head?
25. Shackles
27. Actor married to Demi Moore
32. Make the grade
33. Latest thing
34. Two-time link
37. What surfers hang
38. Viper poison
39. For mature audiences
41. All even
42. Clayton Moore's best-known role
46. Get dirty
47. Word after "see no" or "hear no"
48. ET's vehicle
49. Itchings
50. Light touches
51. Giants' grp.

DOWN

1. ___ de mer (seasickness)
2. Hitter's stat
3. Inning to stretch in
4. One way to walk on water?
5. Salad fish
6. Subjoin
7. Excluded
8. Start for a playwright
9. Log-splitting device
10. First digital computer
11. Office transcriptionist
16. And others too numerous to mention
17. Occurrence
20. Ewe in "Babe"
21. Establishment
22. Pest-control company
25. Trained
26. Sun shade
28. Show up
29. Pistol
30. It may need boosting
31. Dreamer's abbr.
34. Bohemian
35. California lake resort
36. Had a pizza delivered, say
38. Little glass vessels
40. Right-angle joints
41. Nickname for a Chicago newspaper
43. Actress Gabor
44. Fire starter?
45. Giant bird of lore

Answers on page 179.

Fencing Off

ACROSS

1. Gel
4. Somewhat
8. Wiener schnitzel meat
12. TV ET
13. Bupkis, in Bogota
14. ___ dixit
15. "Keep your cool"
17. Old video format
18. Fencer's time-out?
20. Insects with narrow waists
23. 1988 Dennis Quaid/ Meg Ryan movie
24. Bandage brand
25. Insect attracted by salt
30. Fencer's match recount?
33. Cooperation
34. "Silent Spring" topic
35. It's moved in limbo
36. ___ nova (1960s dance)
38. Fencer's attorney?
43. Pool color
44. Common restaurant request
48. Ladder section
49. Adroit
50. Old Roman greeting
51. Flying box?
52. Greek restaurant offering
53. Talk show topic

DOWN

1. Joke
2. Cheer for a bullfighter
3. Repeatedly, in rhyme
4. Breed of cattle
5. Silo neighbor
6. "That's cool, man"
7. Sound system component
8. Amplifier effect
9. Sword with a guarded tip
10. "The Thin Man" terrier
11. News story source, perhaps
16. Austrian peak
19. Old UK airline
20. Steam engine developer
21. Be sore
22. Evening on Mt. Etna
25. Raging
26. Two-player card game
27. Future blooms
28. Loaf parts
29. Sundance's heartthrob
31. Offense
32. Dominion
36. Show respect, maybe
37. ___ binge
38. Gearshift position
39. Here, in Havana
40. Little litter critter
41. ___-deucy
42. Brand, in a way
45. Profs' aides
46. Early evictee
47. Actor Harrison

Answers on page 179.

Balancing Act

ACROSS
1. Between open and closed
5. Crazy in the cabeza
9. Unhappy
12. Dairyland structure
13. "The company for women"
14. Deux preceder
15. Till the ground
16. Proving ground
18. Playground equipment
20. Article written by Germans
21. Some houses are built on it
22. Jack or jenny
25. Name in a 1973 Supreme Court decision
27. Puts away the groceries
30. Child's toys that could be used for jousting practice
34. Chimney passageway
35. Guy's honey
36. Bus. card no.
37. Camera attachment
40. Slangy throw
42. Moment when the unique becomes common
47. Factor in college admissions
48. Gung-ho quality
50. Tree-ring indication
51. "Silver Spoons" actress Gray
52. Office directive
53. Curtain holder
54. Salespeople
55. Some Ben Jonson works

DOWN
1. Type of viper
2. Drop a beau abruptly
3. Soothing houseplant
4. Manned the oars
5. Not right now
6. Above
7. Business expenses
8. In the lead
9. What travelers check?
10. Get the pot started
11. Timid forest creature
17. Grab the wheel
19. Garr or Polo
22. Peke's squeak
23. Scale tone
24. Worked with marble, maybe
26. Heckler's missile
28. Cowboy's moniker
29. Scrapped airplane
31. You can play for it
32. Comes about
33. Butter substitute
38. Less naughty
39. Make noise in bed
41. Gadget
42. Former Russian ruler
43. "Aladdin" parrot voiced by Gilbert Gottfried
44. Traveling bag
45. Sine qua non
46. Broken
49. ___ Altos, Calif.

Answers on page 179.

Sew You Say

ACROSS

1. Last letter
4. 1,760 yards
8. Cherokee maker
12. Devour
13. Banded gemstone
14. Part of QED
15. Coffee server
16. Fed
17. Italy's old capital?
18. Seattle landmark
21. Toothpaste ingredient
22. A little light?
23. Canton's place
26. No. 2's
27. You can't get one if you ground into a DP
30. Be at risk
34. Call yours
35. "Robin Hood: ___ in Tights"
36. Blown-out style
37. Leather worker's tool
38. Cooking amt.
40. Broadcast when off the air
45. Three of a kind beats it
47. Yemen Gate locale
48. Sadness
49. "Circle Game" songwriter Mitchell
50. Very black
51. Paris "yes"
52. Hebrides island
53. Costner played him in 1987
54. "Jeopardy!" phenomenon Jennings

DOWN

1. Father of Helen of Troy
2. Costner played him in 1994
3. European volcano
4. It talks, in a saying
5. Ludicrous
6. Minstrel's strings
7. Selected passage
8. Sweet bread spread
9. One of the Great Lakes
10. Corn serving
11. Harper Valley org. of song
19. Plumber's challenge
20. Recipe guesstimate
23. "What have we here!"
24. "Hee ___!"
25. Room renter
26. Aerostar, e.g.
27. Red card issuer
28. Cantina
29. Courtroom vow
31. M3 and Z3
32. Russia's first president
33. Paying full attention
37. Cliff dwelling
38. Armored vehicles
39. Doesn't flee
40. Pint-sized
41. Window division
42. Creature from the forest moon of Endor
43. Playboy
44. German denial
45. Sleepover attire
46. Fine, to NASA

Answers on page 180.

Films of 1941

ACROSS

1. Lament from Germany
4. Frisbee producer
9. Hoo-ha
12. Prefix with nuptial
13. Sultan's group of wives
14. Women's ___
15. 1941 Cary Grant–Irene Dunne tearjerker
18. Add some booze to
19. Main points
20. Scrape by
23. Tear dryer
24. Pleasant
26. Improvise with the band
27. 1941 Orson Welles classic
31. Unreturned service
32. Goose egg
33. With it
35. Weather line
40. Job seeker's success
41. Telegram
42. 1941 Humphrey Bogart mystery, with "The"
47. Male friend
48. Valentine's Day symbol
49. Frequent ER visitor
50. Match, in poker
51. "Ode on a Grecian Urn" poet
52. Father figures

DOWN

1. Honeycrisp, e.g.
2. Floorboard sound
3. As a result
4. "How come?"
5. Gets a hold of
6. "___ you out of your mind?"
7. Ile surrounder
8. Alpha's opposite
9. One who thinks there's no place like Nome?
10. Served a stretch
11. Beyond zaftig
16. Modern
17. Japanese fighter
21. Lead-in for verse or cycle
22. State of excitement
23. Artist Rousseau
25. Middle grade
27. Token, perhaps
28. Polar bear's resting site
29. View
30. Puts on the floor, briefly
33. Pyramids, essentially
34. Worthless stuff
36. Pooh's feathered friend
37. Flexor muscle, informally
38. Taste stimulus
39. Flat rates?
43. Bring an action against
44. Green org.
45. Tailor's concern
46. Magazine thickeners

Answers on page 180.

Winter Wonders

ACROSS

1. "It ___ a very good year"
4. Resistance units
8. Rich topsoil
12. Picnic pest
13. Gather, as grain
14. Otherwise
15. Fun winter "battle": 2 wds.
18. Mama's mate
19. Letter opener?
20. Sailor's assent
21. "Hee ___"
23. Gratuity
25. Chicken ___ king: 2 wds.
28. Service station purchase
30. Big faux pas
34. Athletes on the ice: 2 wds.
37. Durable alloy
38. Nevertheless
39. It's over an I
40. Precious stone
42. "…___ the land of the free…"
44. Airport abbr.
47. Suds maker
49. Your mom's sister
53. In some homes, this is a winter tradition: 2 wds.
56. Agitate
57. Beginner
58. Fed. property overseer
59. River to the Caspian Sea
60. Auto pioneer Ransom Eli
61. Kind of curve

DOWN

1. Bee's cousin
2. "___ and the King of Siam"
3. "Cut it out!"
4. Spherical body
5. Progress
6. Like about half of us
7. Water balloon sound
8. Oahu garland
9. Olympic gymnast Korbut
10. Pasty-faced
11. Parcel (out)
16. Baby's bawl
17. Warship
22. Eternal
24. Settle, as a debt
25. Contented sighs
26. Fate
27. Sharpshooter
29. Mata Hari, for example
31. Provided with sustenance
32. To and ___
33. Winter hrs. in Boston
35. Beer barrel
36. Large, spotted cat
41. Phrase on a coat of arms
43. Pied Piper follower
44. Hosiery shade
45. Norse god of thunder
46. Diva's big song
48. ___ nitrate
50. Egg on
51. Loch of note
52. Afternoon socials
54. Under the weather
55. "Mayday!"

Answers on page 180.

International Headlines

ACROSS

1. Writing tablets
5. Stylish
9. Excellent, sl.
13. Sad news item
14. Gossipy Barrett
15. Plumb crazy
16. Angry Emerald Isle residents brooded?
19. Mil. address
20. Domicile: abbr.
21. 1962 hit subtitled "That Kiss!"
22. Old-fashioned business letter salutation
24. Beauty pageant toppers
26. "One Flew Over the Cuckoo's Nest" author
28. British WWII-era gun
29. Flounder's cousin
33. ___ Angeles
35. "___ while we're on the subject…"
36. He killed Abel
37. Generous Holland folks provided dinner?
42. Prefix with space or dynamic
43. "Gotcha!"
44. ___ or nothing
45. Metric weight
46. Moolah
48. Bloodsucker
52. "___ Place," 1957 Lana Turner movie
54. Have the nerve
55. Amber-colored beer
59. Pro bono ad: abbr.
61. Census category
62. Parisians wilted last summer?
65. Aide: abbr.
66. Govt. home financing org.
67. Folk singer Guthrie
68. Topers
69. Part of an udder
70. Low voice

DOWN

1. Common TV dinner
2. Absolutely despises
3. Gaming cube
4. Mix, as cake batter
5. Crucial situation
6. Santa's syllables
7. Intrinsic
8. Prophetess of Greek myth
9. Commoner: abbr.
10. Sewing machine inventor Elias
11. Scores 100 percent
12. Kind of list
17. Eligible for a pension, maybe: abbr.
18. How-___ (helpful books)
19. Inquire
23. Rarely
25. Stopped
27. "I love ___"
29. Climbed, as a mountain
30. Feedbag morsel
31. Prevaricate
32. Termination
34. Play director's exit destination
37. "You're it!" chasing game
38. That girl
39. Pitcher's stat
40. Native American Montana people
41. Pipe joint
47. Formal headgear
49. Painters' stands
50. Principle statements
51. Evil spell
52. ___ for the course
53. Letters on a bounced check
55. School orgs.
56. "I see," facetiously
57. "___ we forget"
58. Small salamanders
60. Swift, compact horse
63. Nashville-based awards org.
64. Bank nest egg, initially

Answers on page 180.

Treed

ACROSS

1. Foot in verse
5. Glades
10. Murray and West
14. Bar follower
15. "Middlemarch" author
16. Jerez jar
17. Handle, for Horace
18. Lobo: 2 wds.
20. Prescribed amounts
22. Balzac's "Le ___ Goriot"
23. Woods's prop
24. Pert lass
26. Gallaudet beneficiary
28. Unmarried male
32. Pumice
36. Seraglios
37. Chemical ending
38. Inclination
39. Muralist José Maria
40. Gambled
43. Drat!
44. Athenian demagogue
46. Cicero's "Where?"
47. Rational
48. Minor Persian despot
50. Bridged
52. Dutch export
54. Conservative: abbr.
55. Southern state: abbr.
58. Part of a geom. sign-off
60. Old magistrates
64. Exponents in higher math
67. Fast time
68. "Jeopardy!" host, to friends
69. Caravansary
70. Freeway portion
71. Created
72. Time periods
73. Fillip

DOWN

1. Hussein's former land
2. Japanese aborigine
3. "Wild Horse ___" (Grey)
4. Mercantile subsidiary: 2 wds.
5. Assigned
6. Samuel's counselor
7. Flaccid
8. Like oak leaves
9. Metrical measures
10. Cut grass
11. Thanks ___: 2 wds.
12. She: Fr.
13. Ump's call
19. Respond
21. "___ Kiss": Rodin
25. Morrison, of literature
27. Old Wimbledon rival: 2 wds.
28. Autumn pears
29. Miss St. John
30. Editor's mark
31. Like some gems
33. Stately
34. Jejune
35. Used an abacus
41. Zaragoza's river
42. Diacritical mark
45. Consumer advocate
49. Congregation
51. Norm: abbr.
53. San ___, CA
55. Hoax
56. Manilow's girl of song
57. Matured
59. NY type way
61. Spare
62. Sicilian resort
63. Child or ladder
65. Bunyan's tool
66. Cover with graffiti

Comic Hero to Movie Star

ACROSS

1. "Pimp My Ride" network
4. Whole note's lack
8. PC key
12. Split ___ soup
13. County seat of Allen County, Kansas
14. Mandolin kin
15. Classical language of India
17. Karenina of literature
18. Comic book hero played by Nicolas Cage
20. Bunch of feathers
23. Jungle queen of comics
24. ___ -Locka, Florida
25. Made changes to
28. Comic book hero played by Sylvester Stallone, with 31-Across
31. See 28-Across
32. Make go
35. PBS funder
36. Blunt
38. Loads of
39. Comic book hero played by Dick Durock
42. Minnesota neighbor
43. Circles
47. Gillette's ___ II razor
48. "Catch!"
49. Biol. evidence
50. Scottish island
51. Belgian river
52. Quaint

DOWN

1. Army arresters: abbr.
2. Brewed beverage
3. Airport-shuttle vehicle
4. Follower of Guru Nanak
5. Bullfight competitors
6. Bible prophet
7. Barbie's company
8. Less ornate
9. Former home of the Cleveland Cavaliers
10. "___ Reader" (eclectic magazine)
11. Bartlett or Anjou
16. Warrant officer's inferior: abbr.
19. No longer in service: abbr.
20. Japanese WWII general
21. Start of a Fifth Dimension tune or a Superman departure
22. Gradually disappeared
26. The first garden
27. WWII turning point
29. Possible reaction to bad news
30. Tombstone lawman Wyatt
33. Easily annoyed
34. Reverberates
37. Solution strength, in Surrey
38. Joe Torre, e.g.: abbr.
39. Joins a jury
40. Function
41. Poetic negative
44. A bachelor's last words?
45. Conclude
46. Bummed out

Answers on page 181.

Funny Guys

ACROSS

1. Some office workers
6. Drillmaster's syllable
9. Potato chip flavor
12. Not in the dark
13. 1983 film romance "___ Jeunesse"
14. Future swimmers
15. Holdover
16. Crankiness
18. Kind of therapy
20. "I Don't Know Why" singer
21. Sondheim's Sweeney
22. Cartoon response to a punch
25. ___ degree
27. Indebted to
30. Holiday mail
34. Porky Pig, e.g.
35. Writer Tan
36. Sure thing
37. Suggest
40. Miner's find
42. "Superman" costar
47. Film cut
48. "Beggars can't be choosers," e.g.
49. "Kiss my grits" utterer
50. Tail fastener, in a party game
51. Kind of battery: abbr.
52. Frustum-shape hat
53. Wolf down
54. Grass beginnings

DOWN

1. Grounds cover
2. Vessel for Aquarius
3. Its capital is Bamaki
4. First-class, in slang
5. Trigonometric ratios
6. Busy centers
7. Set into motion
8. Cy Young Award winner Martinez
9. Theatrical row
10. More than an uptick
11. Conclusion, in a proof
17. French wine region
19. Sack
22. St. Crispin's Day mo.
23. "I know what you're up to!"
24. Totally
26. Whom the SG addresses
28. "... ___ the set of sun" ("Macbeth")
29. Cavity filler's deg.
31. Lifeless
32. Crazed
33. Aleppo residents
38. Hardly poker-faced
39. Mobile phone maker
41. Jack Russell terrier on "Frasier"
42. Army mascot
43. Army shelter
44. Carp's kin
45. Old-style "Holy cow!"
46. Wine list column
47. Not one's normal self

Answers on page 181.

Cover Up

ACROSS

1. Inn, briefly
6. Lady Bird's monogram
9. Distant
12. Greek meeting place
13. Draft pick?
14. Iron man's quest?
15. Lowest point
16. Negative conjunction
17. Not working
18. Award given to the Masters golf tournament winner
21. Caviar source
22. It stands for something
25. Kreskin's forte
28. "Superman" actor Beatty
30. Mother of Jesus
31. High school attire
35. Thieves' undoer Ali ____
36. Tyler of "Armageddon"
37. Gardening tool
38. Fire station fixtures
41. Michelle Obama, ____ Robinson
43. Fad of the 1920s
48. Daily riser
50. Vulcan or Vishnu
51. Dog
52. Oxlike antelope
53. Fleecy female
54. Highest-ranking, in some hierarchies
55. Male turkey
56. Chicago rides
57. Button for bowlers

DOWN

1. Military report
2. Culture contents
3. Joint point
4. Less humid
5. Without exception
6. Turner of Tinseltown
7. Voting groups
8. Dried beef product
9. Relief for sore tootsies
10. Cousin of "woof!"
11. Call, as a game: abbr.
19. Mock
20. Anthony's costar in "Remains of the Day" and "Howards End"
23. Nabisco cookie
24. Greek harp
25. Exile island for Napoleon
26. Easter or Christmas stamp
27. "There's a sucker born every minute" speaker
29. Broadband connection, briefly
32. O'Hara estate
33. Ripple tippler
34. How some golfers shoot a round
39. John D. MacDonald sleuth Travis ____
40. Look like a sourpuss
42. French academy
44. Old-fashioned poems
45. Cousin of "uh-oh"
46. Massage target
47. "____ '70s Show"
48. NCO on a drill
49. Kids' card game

Answers on page 181.

Fruit Salad

ACROSS

1. Rivers of comedy
5. Collect
10. Tabloid mention
14. Exile isle
15. Programming language
16. Writer/director Ephron
17. Larynx part
19. Publicist's concern
20. Certain Asian Americans
21. "My boy…"
22. Word in old matrimonial rites
23. Lady dealing in futures?
26. 1965 march site
28. Pry
30. Browning work
33. Mule of song
36. Exodus figure
38. Baby grand, perhaps?
39. Old TV's "___ Three Lives"
41. Kind of code
43. Quotation notation
44. Half of 1960s quartet
46. Reporter's coup
48. Bass, for one
49. Cue
51. Inbox contents
53. ___ Ark

55. Deadlock
59. Soapstone component
61. "Boola-Boola" singer
63. Ties up
64. Airline since 1948
65. Midday appointments, maybe
68. Actor Rob of "Masquerade"
69. Gates licensed it to IBM in 1981
70. Vaquero's weapon
71. Not as much
72. Gives ___ (cares)
73. Sole

DOWN

1. Denims
2. Nostalgic number
3. Humiliate
4. Stoolies, sometimes
5. Lawyers' org.
6. It'll give you a sense of direction
7. They're filled with venom
8. Missile shelters
9. Play parts
10. Sleepless state
11. Project head
12. Pennsylvania port
13. Lots of
18. Saint Catherine's hometown

24. Ivory bar?
25. Wounds
27. An arborist might do it
29. ___ de Leon
31. Organic compound
32. Pitch
33. Fool
34. Winged
35. Vehicle buyers' protection
37. "Whither thou goest" addressee
40. Ancient Greek associated with a sword
42. Good earth
45. Upscale bath feature
47. Spoke (up)
50. Louise's film friend
52. Certain washbowl
54. Sloppy snow
56. Saint Elizabeth Ann ___
57. Fishhook line
58. English class assignment
59. Relate
60. African succulent
62. ___-European
66. Emulate a pigeon
67. Marshall Plan implementer's monogram

Answers on page 182.

Colorful Clues

ACROSS

1. What Wednesday's child is full of
4. TV comedian Carey
8. Jupiter has a big red one
12. Shanty
13. Solemn vow
14. Last item in Pandora's box
15. First person in Germany
16. Tubular pasta
17. Cajun thickener
18. Yellow Book listings
21. Quasimodo portrayer Chaney
22. Bear's foot
23. Comic book cry of pain
25. Skater's jump
27. South Korean automaker
30. Little black book listings
33. Pig shelter
34. Elbows in pipe
35. Not so much
36. Metro maker
37. Matador's support
38. Blue book listing
44. Small songbird
45. Female friend in France
46. Poison ___
47. Words of comparison
48. Nashville is its capital: abbr.
49. Born
50. Org. with a shuttle program
51. Football positions
52. Word after natural or tear

DOWN

1. Party line enforcer
2. Cry of pain
3. Study of behavior
4. Typical roses order
5. Gutter filler
6. "___, Brute?"
7. Cries softly
8. She needed taming, according to Shakespeare
9. Start of Ben Franklin's almanac?
10. ___ Dei
11. Cowboy nickname
19. Start of a bedtime prayer
20. Indonesian island
23. "You are correct, sir!"
24. Phone line abbr.
25. Distribute according to plan
26. Org. that played for one season in 2001
27. Position of prayer
28. Driver's license and the like, abbr.
29. Beast of burden
31. "Walk on the Wild Side" singer Lou
32. Jazz singer Fitzgerald
36. Birthplace of Italian poet Eugenio Montale
37. Kilns
38. Stellar bear
39. Drops below the horizon
40. The last word in churches?
41. Cacao pod covering
42. Layer of the iris
43. They may be peeled
44. Victory

Answers on page 182.

About Face

ACROSS

1. Intended course
5. Leaf of grass
10. Practice boxing
14. No friend to Othello
15. Hammerin' Hank
16. Superman's childhood pal Lang
17. Bancroft-MacLaine film: 3 wds.
20. In order
21. Be in accord
22. Cravats
23. Marketplaces in ancient Rome
25. Riding clothes
28. Exacts
31. South Seas romance of 1847
32. Greased
33. Narrow inlet
35. Novel by John Marquand: 4 wds.
39. Spring collectors: abbr.
40. Eroded
41. "Planet of the ___"
42. Calmed with medication
44. Ancient Palestinian fortress
46. Organization: abbr.
47. Sing with great force
48. Look fixedly
51. Snakes
55. Lets the heat in: 4 wds.
58. Poker stake
59. Of space
60. Speedy animal
61. Film holder
62. "Funny Girl" Brice
63. Sea eagle

DOWN

1. Bread used in the East
2. The Cowardly Lion actor
3. Land in Caesar's day
4. Memo
5. Flat-bottomed boats
6. Bowling alleys
7. Parched
8. Knotts
9. School subject: abbr.
10. "I Like Ike," e.g.
11. Two of a kind
12. Bancroft or Boleyn
13. Evaluate
18. Part of a military group
19. Thanksgiving Day event
23. Wrong-doer
24. Hebrew measure
25. Mesa dwellers
26. Cupids in paintings
27. Capital of Idaho
28. Broke bread
29. Mountain dweller of Tibet
30. Begot
32. Many times
34. Handle: Lat.
36. Raises the nap
37. Fare for Dobbin
38. "___ luxury of woe" (Thomas Moore): 2 wds.
43. Type of grass
44. Just
45. Paradise for skiers
47. Irish playwright
48. Play the lead
49. Choreographer Tommy
50. Comedian Johnson
51. British carbine
52. At hand
53. Mountain lake
54. Pintail duck
56. Blockhead
57. Gun owners group: abbr.

Answers on page 182.

Start of Something Big

ACROSS

1. Pizzeria need
5. Kindergarten stuff
9. Circus cry
12. Plain writing
13. "Darn it all!"
14. Michigan in Chicago: abbr.
15. Longing
16. Bad habit and then some
17. Bit of wry laughter
18. Worthless bit
19. Subject of US patent #223898
21. Winter gear
23. Suffix with Brooklyn
24. Comes up with something
27. Humane grp.
31. Tournament favorite
34. Ballpark near LaGuardia Airport
35. Diversified
36. Merino's hangout
39. Labor
40. Health food store purchase
44. Veto
47. Wall St. rating
48. Circle dance
49. Specialized mag
50. Beta follower
51. Gray area?: abbr.
52. Rounded hairdo
53. "Go team!"
54. Wall St. letters
55. Part of a hammer head

DOWN

1. Milo's partner in a 1989 movie
2. Presidential prerogative
3. Polite words of interruption
4. Highest degree?
5. Counselor
6. Kind of general: abbr.
7. Hidden trove
8. Manuscript markings
9. Site of Interstate H1
10. Speedskater's path
11. Oregano, e.g.
19. Low in calories
20. Truman and Myerson
22. 1967 talking board game
24. Powerful bunch
25. Moron's comment
26. Spread, as seed
28. Quill cutter, once
29. Lincoln center?
30. Recipe word
32. Hot dog ingredient
33. Dutch cheese
37. Revolutionary War hero Allen
38. Anguish
40. Full of ripples
41. Comic's reward
42. 1977 hit for the Commodores
43. Pitcher's figs.
45. Memo subject header
46. An Intel microprocessor
49. Irradiate

Answers on page 182.

If You Want to Get Technical

ACROSS

1. "There ___ for the grace..."
4. Less than twice
8. Movie about a great white
12. Had pizza, say
13. Kind of fence
14. Without delay, on memos
15. November veggie
16. For dieters
17. Shetland ___
18. Cthulhu Mythos creator
21. French article
22. X can mean this
23. Salt may add it
26. Significant period of time
27. By way of
30. Wonder Woman was one
34. Young yipper
35. "The Tell-Tale Heart" author
36. Word from a pen
37. "___ boom bah!"
38. Org. for drivers
40. Saint Louis landmark
45. Sonora snack
46. Raw silk's color
47. Rowboat accessory
49. Green beginner?
50. Communicant's response
51. "___ Framed Roger Rabbit"
52. Study furniture
53. Communicate via PDA
54. Wee boy

DOWN

1. Prolonged howl
2. Six-sided state
3. Holiday hire
4. Durable synthetic
5. Simple
6. Call upon
7. Sibling to Iphigeneia, Chrysothemis, and Orestes
8. Island nation
9. Starting from
10. Would like
11. Secret agent
19. Skating jump
20. Caboose position
23. Use the microwave
24. Down-under bird
25. Sticky stuff from a tree
26. Farm mother
27. Number of articles in the Constitution
28. It may be negative or positive
29. Flood insurance?
31. Young Taylor on TV
32. "Piece of cake!"
33. Crowd sound
37. Long-legged bird
38. Cookware brand
39. Thin and angular
40. Contributed
41. Flying experts
42. Wile E. Coyote's supply company
43. Hooded garment
44. Oft-sarcastic utterance
45. "How I Met Your Mother" narrator
48. Engine part

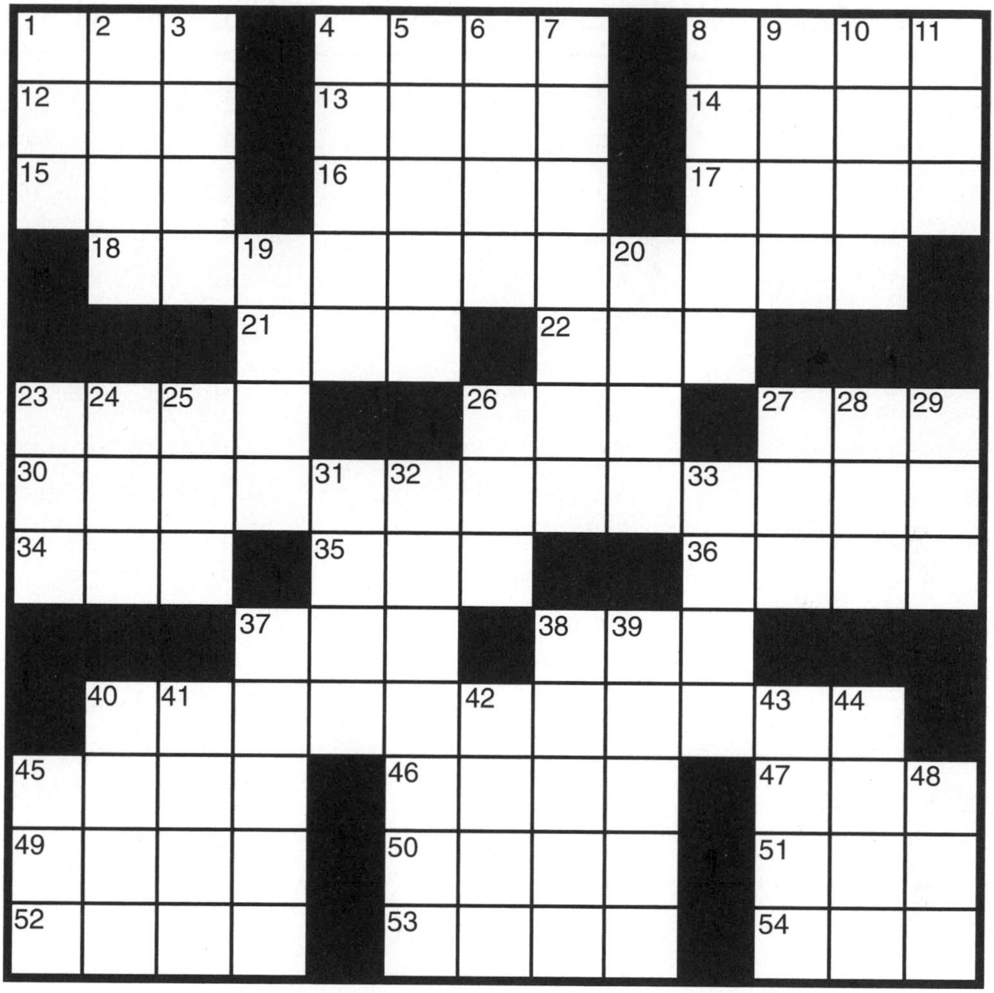

Answers on page 183.

Playing Post Office

ACROSS

1. Wine barrel
5. Gold-related
10. Inevitable destruction
14. Comrade in arms
15. Spanish silver
16. Aptly named tropical fruit
17. Language not used in polite society
20. Spooky
21. Asian nursemaid
22. Contractor's quote: abbr.
23. Omelet ingredients
26. Put one's foot down?
28. Dashboard meas.
31. Fireworks reactions
33. Peaceful
37. ___ the Red
39. Spinning toys
41. Districted
42. Exceed accepted limits
45. Be crazy about
46. Plumlike gin flavoring
47. Distinctive flair
48. Desired answer to "Are you going to help me?"
50. Lane of the "Daily Planet"
52. Capone and Gore
53. Garbage barge
55. Implore
57. School of thought: suffix
60. River to the Caspian Sea
62. Gather up
66. Official okay
70. Winter Olympics sledding event
71. Mexican mister
72. Infamous Roman emperor
73. Shorten text, perhaps
74. Clear the chalkboard
75. Grasp firmly

DOWN

1. Sidewalk eatery
2. Skin cream additive
3. Insulting remark
4. ___ eleison ("Lord, have mercy")
5. Gorilla, for one
6. Final: abbr.
7. Pro ___
8. Tabloid twosomes
9. Gem units
10. Close pair
11. Monster
12. Auto pioneer Ransom Eli
13. Spray
18. Toy block brand
19. Breathe laboriously
24. Fourth-century invader
25. Loafers and oxfords
27. Laboring class member
28. Satisfy, as a loan
29. Priggish one
30. Japanese soup flavorings
32. Compete in a bee
34. Bomber ___ Gay
35. Katmandu's land
36. Ideal places
38. Evert of tennis
40. Nosy one
43. It sits in a saucer
44. Bride's head covering
49. In a glum mood
51. Scorch
54. Small thin cookie
56. Surrounded by
57. ___ of Wight
58. Type of poker game
59. Crèche figures
61. Turner the actress
63. Allege
64. Garment for a rani
65. Pig's dinner
67. Was introduced to
68. Not neg.
69. Opposite of post

Answers on page 183.

Merry Christmas

ACROSS

1. ___ 'n' roll music
5. ___-ovo vegetarian
10. Frosts a cake
14. Press, as a laundered shirt
15. Take ___ for the worse: 2 wds.
16. Loathsome
17. Genealogical chart: 2 wds.
19. New Haven school
20. Makes very happy
21. ___-Tzu (Taoism founder)
22. Bank offering
23. Swedish car
25. Adjust, as a piano
27. Alphabetical introduction
30. Q-Tip, e.g.
32. Copied, in a way
36. Auto warmer: 2 wds.
39. Ancient Greek marketplace
40. Award for best ad
41. Affirmatives
43. ___ Bator (Mongolia's capital)
44. Lively dances
46. Miniature sculpture
48. Confuses
50. "Shoo!"
51. "Mayday!"
52. Feminine org. since 1855
54. End of the work wk. cry
56. Ship's personnel
59. World Series mo.
61. Parisian places of learning
65. Model anew
66. Film director's cry after a successful take: 3 wds.
68. The "A" in A.D.
69. Hip joints: ECO AX anagram
70. Misplace
71. Sweat unit
72. Raise with a crane
73. Snick and ___

DOWN

1. Widespread
2. By mouth
3. Extremely deep sleep
4. Makes booties, maybe
5. Uses a certain store payment plan: 2 wds.
6. Court figure: abbr.
7. Hair ringlet
8. "Trick or ___!"
9. Early inning status: 2 wds.
10. Association including Harvard and Princeton: 2 wds.
11. "Ta-ta, Antonio!"
12. Jazzy Fitzgerald
13. Spotted
18. Renter's document
24. Motel in "Psycho"
26. Second Amendment rights grp.
27. Ghana's capital
28. Bundled, as hay
29. Wept
31. Outdoes
33. Young male horses
34. Poet's muse
35. Copenhagen natives
37. Los Angeles movie center
38. Giggle when tickled, say
42. Broadway assembly: 2 wds.
45. Use a Singer
47. Central New York city on the Mohawk
49. Type of whiskey
53. Sneeze sound

55. Chickens and ducks, e.g.
56. Seafood choice
57. Philosopher Descartes
58. ___ St. Vincent Millay
60. Cab
62. Scientology's ___ Hubbard
63. Leisure
64. World War I German admiral
67. Prof's helpers

Answers on page 183.

Carrying On

ACROSS
1. Ring
5. Mardi ___
9. Do a Thanksgiving dinner job
14. Bear constellation
15. River past Buckingham
16. Foreign
17. Competitions with forwards and guards
20. SASE, e.g.
21. "For shame!"
22. Cookie-selling org.
25. "Tommy" rock opera group: 2 wds.
27. "I ___ Little Prayer for You": 2 wds.
31. Holler
33. Quite pale
34. Retired prof's title
35. Actress Normand of the silents
37. Brunch time, maybe
39. Saint Patrick's Day parade participant, likely: 2 wds.
42. Provided funds for, as a car loan
43. Facial features
45. ___ the Red
46. China's Zhou ___

49. Alternative magazine founded in 1984
50. 6/6/44
51. The highest volcano in Eur.
53. Gridiron gains: abbr.
54. Poetic meadow
55. Gambler's figures
57. Facially expressing disapproval, perhaps: 3 wds.
65. Small musical combos
66. "The Virginian" author Wister
67. State settled by Brigham Young
68. Apprehension
69. Tree home?
70. Like many a horror film

DOWN
1. Place to get a Guinness
2. Memorable period
3. Ninny
4. Fresh body of water
5. "Aha!"
6. Russian coins
7. Botanist Gray
8. Bookstore section: hyph.
9. Parakeet's place

10. ___ mode: 2 wds.
11. Edge
12. Churchill's sign
13. Coast Guard rank: abbr.
18. Treebeard in "The Lord of the Rings," e.g.
19. Big name in model trains
22. Phys. ed. class locale
23. Gull or tern
24. Tirane's country
26. Cajole
27. "Ciao!": 2 wds.
28. General pardon
29. Accountant's closing time: 2 wds.
30. Hand and shoulder connector
32. Inheritance
36. Hospital staffer: abbr.
38. Moving vehicle
40. Bygone block deliverers
41. It has five sides
42. Gave sustenance
44. French possessive pronoun
47. Observes Yom Kippur
48. Tab key function
52. Commercials

98

54. It might be headed "To Do"
56. Fake vending machine coin
57. School group: abbr.
58. Big coffee server
59. 18-wheeler
60. "Mayday!"
61. Be in arrears
62. "How was ___ know?": 2 wds.
63. Golfer's standard
64. Timid

Answers on page 183.

Awfully Nice

ACROSS

1. Korea's continent
5. Napoleon's isle of exile
9. Wedding party transports
14. Shellac ingredients
15. Refrigerate
16. "___ ___ a Parade"
17. Fill-in for a talk show, e.g.
19. Chimney channels
20. Dress, as a judge
21. "Ditto"
23. Imp
24. Got up
25. Decompose
27. London cathedral
31. Mexican money
35. Forty winks
37. Bisects
38. Strong glue
40. Teacher's favorite
42. Explosive experiment, for short
43. Colored anew
45. Hit with a stun gun
47. Panamas and boaters
48. Joins forces (with)
50. Practical joke
52. "___ ___ mio!"
54. Search parties, in the Old West
59. Retaliation
62. Geritol target
63. Mistake
64. "Heavens!"
66. Skirt style
67. Until
68. "I cannot tell ___ ___"
69. Singer/actress Della
70. Fair hiring org.
71. Big wigs in biz

DOWN

1. Horatio of inspirational books
2. Spa spot
3. Bakery employees
4. Org.
5. Level of authority
6. Toilet, in London
7. "Blame it on the ___ Nova"
8. Sanctuary centerpieces
9. Threescore and ten, maybe
10. Sickness
11. Pout
12. Finished
13. Ousted Zaire ruler Mobuto ___ Seko
18. Way up the ski slope
22. Wool-eating insect
26. Faucet
28. Middle layer of the eye
29. "___ we forget"
30. Grounded sound breakers: abbr.
31. Saucy, as a young lass
32. Pointless fencing sword
33. Fountain treat
34. What 17 Across, 64 Across, 10 Down, and this puzzle's title are
36. Dispenser candy
39. "You betcha!"
41. "You're it!" chasing game
44. Performing twosomes
46. One time Haitian dictator, informally
49. One of ten in Exodus
51. Bell hit with a hammer
53. Wed on the run
55. Glacial ridge
56. Photographer's request
57. Old MacDonald's refrain
58. Bank vaults
59. Back side
60. ___ Stanley Gardner
61. ___-dieu (prayer bench)
65. Oklahoma Native American

Answers on page 184.

Panagram

In this crossword puzzle, every letter of the alphabet is used at least once.

ACROSS

1. Is apparently
6. Teen's "Yeah, right!"
10. Apparel
14. "...who ___ heaven": 2 wds.
15. Swiss hero William
16. Skin moisturizer
17. Proof of car ownership
18. Ward of "Sisters"
19. Techie workplaces, often
20. Applied pressure to
22. Moon stages
24. Kind of code or rug
25. Comet alternative
26. Barely burned
29. Animal with a duck bill
33. Shout of encouragement
34. Streisand's "Funny Girl" role
35. One-million link
36. Tattered attire
37. Disreputable doctor
38. Move like a hummingbird
39. Fruit-drink suffix
40. "I Remember Mama" actress Irene
41. Plundered treasure
42. Nonconformist
44. Intermediate weight boxer, for short
45. Corleone's creator
46. Notorious pirate captain
47. Wings it
50. Alluded to
54. Swamp reptile, for short
55. Burglar's take
57. Tater state
58. Simba's love, in "The Lion King"
59. Hershiser of baseball
60. Wrapped movie monster
61. Series ending
62. Money rolls
63. Fencing blades

DOWN

1. College entrance exams
2. "ER" actor La Salle
3. Words to Brutus
4. Odometer readings
5. Scoffing sort
6. Totally befuddled
7. Sunflower edible
8. Not in the pink
9. Pancake
10. Large collection of stars
11. Wistful word
12. Dressing gown
13. Porgy's lady
21. Last letter, in Britain
23. Despise
25. Wonderland visitor
26. "Beat it!"
27. "If ___ nickel for every time...": 3 wds.
28. Israeli desert
29. Shenanigan
30. Light in the furnace
31. Link up
32. Mythical reveler
34. Con game
37. "The $64,000 Question," e.g.
38. Went out of business
40. Defeat decisively
41. "Nighty-night" hour
43. Grand in scope
44. Finish first
46. Stops, as a story
47. Teen outbreak
48. Doggone!
49. Whatever she wants, she gets
50. Shaded
51. Title for Judi Dench
52. Sigh words
53. Playthings
56. Coach Parseghian of Notre Dame fame

Answers on page 184.

Animal House

ACROSS

1. Concordes: abbr.
5. Bass and treble
10. Teases
14. Lotion additive
15. Aged: Lat.
16. Concerning: Lat., 2 wds.
17. Biggest portion: 2 wds.
19. Amateur sports group: abbr.
20. Editor's equipment
21. Owl hours
23. Paul, the guitar guy
24. Ready supply
26. Greek physician
29. Exclude
30. ___ plea (pleads guilty): sl., 2 wds.
34. Military address: abbr.
35. Greek flier
38. Pinches
39. Ivy League team: 2 wds.
42. Ireland
43. Fuel vessel
44. Regret
45. Lots and lots: var.
47. Kleindienst, Kennedy, Civiletti, etc.: abbr.
48. Beginning
50. O'Casey and Connery
52. One: Fr.
53. Dan, former CBS newsman
56. Mournful
60. Surrounding atmosphere
61. String game: 2 wds.
64. Put away
65. Wipe out
66. Young adult
67. Make like a goose
68. Put off
69. Orient

DOWN

1. Mineo and Maglie
2. Sales receipt
3. Implement
4. Mentally deteriorated
5. Examples
6. Annealing oven
7. Timetable heading: abbr.
8. Distant
9. Office skill, for short
10. Giant simian: 2 wds.
11. Traverse little by little
12. Mild oath
13. Oceans
18. Like some views
22. Transport watchdogs: abbr.
24. East Indian dresses
25. Ring apparel
26. Stares open mouthed
27. March follower
28. French river
29. WWII battle site
31. Breakwaters
32. Mold opening
33. Plus quality
36. That: Fr.
37. Sault ___ Marie
40. Reporter: 2 wds.
41. Presser
46. Match the bet
49. Nullify
51. Curved
52. Worrier's worry
53. Allergic evidence
54. Manual's companion, for short
55. 1982 animated Disney feature
56. Being: Lat.
57. Concept
58. Pub drinks
59. Penny
62. 100 square meters
63. Make lace

Answers on page 184.

The International Scene

ACROSS

1. Ooze
5. Excuse
10. Soothing ointment
14. Summon
15. A difficulty or complication
16. Double-reed woodwind
17. They're fiercer than city apes: 2 wds.
20. Member speaking for the whole ball team: hyph.
21. Lacks
22. Enola ___
23. Untidy place
24. Performer
27. This gun for hire
33. Central part
34. Military barracks
35. Quilting party, perhaps
36. Countries just hatched: 2 wds.
39. Turn over the engine
40. National song
41. Quote or mention
42. White-collar bag
44. Cuts from copy
45. "___ Were King": 2 wds.

46. Defeater of the Luftwaffe: abbr.
47. Nappy leather
50. Mermaids have them
56. Controlled by the military: 3 wds.
58. German river or dam
59. God's fishbowl
60. Peru's capital
61. Boys
62. Squeeze in
63. Observed

DOWN

1. Atlantic porgy
2. English noble
3. Noted island prison
4. Theater lover: hyph.
5. Quite incensed
6. Turn down: var.
7. Fixe or reçue: Fr.
8. Expel air
9. Middle East country: abbr.
10. Henry's Anne
11. Fit
12. Burden
13. Army meal
18. Close
19. Meaning
23. Beat it!

24. Sharp and biting
25. Person on way to success
26. Famous fountain of Rome
27. Devilfish
28. Baltic natives
29. Opera's Fleming
30. Seething
31. French income
32. Affirmatives
34. Beatrice, "The Beautiful Parricide"
37. Lighting director
38. Chunks dropping off glaciers
43. Downy ducks
44. Computer input or output
46. Class of German wines
47. Takes to court
48. Loosen a knot
49. Happy place
50. Confront
51. Steamed
52. Men only
53. Mr. Nastase
54. Feeble, as an excuse
55. Singer of one last song
57. Shorten the grass

Answers on page 184.

Sevens

ACROSS

1. Gowns
8. Sedative
15. Distributed the deck again
16. Akin
17. Ready, willing, ___: 2 wds.
18. Standing up
19. More tired
20. Speeder's speed, perhaps
21. Queen ___ lace
23. Melody
24. Walks nervously
26. Guiding light
31. Mists
32. Antisocial one
33. One ___ time: 2 wds.
34. Six make an inning
35. Lawn machine
36. Story basis
37. Exploit
38. Paddy crops
39. Monotonous hum
40. Give a second examination
42. Actress Dunne
43. Cinder
44. Sagas
46. Brainier
50. Kitchen appliance
54. Italian dessert
55. Citrus drink
56. Changed
57. Warned
58. Yellowstone attractions
59. Deteriorates

DOWN

1. Sketch
2. Philosopher Descartes
3. Norse epic
4. Some regattas: 2 wds.
5. Roman victims of 290 B.C.
6. Burstyn and DeGeneres
7. Cubic meter
8. Bikini halves
9. He enjoys novels twice
10. Famed portrayer of Hamlet
11. Microwave devices
12. "To put ___ a nutshell...": 2 wds.
13. Impression
14. Nervous
22. Most snaillike
24. Take a short break
25. Mexican native
27. Wallet fillers
28. Claw
29. Make amends
30. Velocity
31. Time unit
32. Door feature
35. Author of "The Covenant"
36. Mangle operators
38. Make like new
39. Visionary
41. Author Bret, et al
42. Philippines city
45. Counselor-___: hyph.
46. Buck
47. Burrower
48. Bohemian
49. Frees (of)
51. London gallery
52. Actress Barbara
53. Ohio team

Answers on page 185.

Gram's Birthday

ACROSS

1. Dangerous when it flows
5. He wrote "The Stars and Stripes Forever"
10. Like a senior citizen
14. Milton wrote them
15. Surrounding atmospheres
16. Sideless cart
17. Small units of weight
19. Unusual
20. Chant
21. Law: Fr.
22. Mean little kids
23. Branch of the service: abbr.
25. Northeastern state of India
27. Enroll
32. Comb. of high cards: 2 wds.
35. The Southwest's Bret
36. Actress Debra
38. Reagan, to friends
39. Ages
40. Sprayed defensively
41. If it's "half," it's small
42. Where to get $$: abbr.
43. Welfare allotments
44. Civil War general
45. Oklahoman
47. Kitchen utensil
49. Showers with stones
51. Eternally: poet.
52. Sound of laughter
54. Once ___ blue moon: 2 wds.
56. Things to eat
61. Smell
62. Heart examination
64. Eat
65. Silkworms
66. Tear down: sp. var.
67. English monetary abbreviation
68. Coarse grass
69. Tennis stadium honoree

DOWN

1. Places
2. Between Yemen and Oman
3. Escape port for air
4. Regarding: 2 wds.
5. Wisest
6. Belonging to us
7. ___ Mountains
8. Where R.L.S. died
9. Helped
10. Name of six popes
11. Parser
12. Wyatt ___
13. Colors
18. Sign on a lab door: 2 wds.
24. Himalayan kingdom
26. Part of a tennis match
27. Flightless SA birds
28. "An ___ the ground": 2 wds.
29. Record player
30. Possessive pronoun
31. "The Camptown ___"
33. Spanish earl
34. "Abandon hope, all ye who ___ here" (Dante)
37. "Beau ___"
40. Tenons' companions
41. Charlottetown is its capital: abbr.
43. Singer Shannon
44. Driver Andretti
46. Closer
48. Edit
50. Trap
52. Devices for carrying bricks
53. Mine entrance
55. Sere
57. Taj Mahal city
58. Depression agencies: abbr.
59. Elan
60. Duck
63. Hammarskjöld

Answers on page 185.

Famous Fare

ACROSS

1. Tortoiselike
5. Word with wrench or dream
9. Medieval weapons
14. Ice shape
15. Yemeni port
16. Actress Verdugo
17. Top draft status
18. Furnish temporarily
19. Wise legislator
20. Beloved TV dairy product?
23. Hosp. areas
24. Voice-man Blanc
25. Pianist Dame Myra
26. Lush surroundings?
27. Nairobi Trio players
29. Howard Hughes's airline
32. Frequently
35. Spread unit
36. Famous twins' birthplace
37. Comedic pastry?
40. Summer coolers
41. Attention-getter
42. Argument flaws
43. Kind of party
44. Tucked in for the night
45. Director's cry
46. The Police was one
48. Norm's bartender
49. Convened
52. Soul food dessert?
57. Pertaining to surface extent
58. Ajar, e.g.
59. Hennery
60. Recipe instruction
61. One side of a 1973 ruling
62. Whet
63. Roman social sites
64. Luge, e.g.
65. Lyric poems

DOWN

1. Twenty
2. Type of month
3. Heeds
4. Don
5. Four-time Masters champ
6. Perfect example
7. Historic Quaker
8. Prefix meaning "inside"
9. Interlocks
10. Fleshy medicinal plants
11. Heavenly
12. Cain's nephew
13. Rational
21. Certain sultanate citizen
22. Root in the stands
26. They must be covered to be real
27. Hurt plenty
28. Spring event
30. Aftermath
31. "My Cup Runneth Over" singer Ed
32. Leave out
33. Confront
34. Doctor's specialty
35. Former Davis Cup captain
36. Glaswegian, e.g.
38. Big shot
39. Tack type
44. Ushers' milieus
45. Sacked
47. Extend
48. Nobel, e.g.
49. Rose
50. Offer reparation
51. Genres
52. Entrance part
53. Diva's piece
54. Spats
55. Fall birthstone
56. Reverberate

Answers on page 185.

Studio 54

ACROSS

1. Spin
7. Partner of pains
12. Complete miss
14. Rake over the coals
15. Makeup of edible Scottie dogs
17. Breakfast partner
18. Act like an icicle?
19. That is, Latin
21. ___ Saint-Louis
22. Onetime BMT rival
23. 2001 International Tennis Hall of Fame inductee
25. Presidential act
26. Sacred place
29. Opposed
31. Denial from Putin
32. Fruit implement
34. Truly, madly, or deeply: abbr.
35. Open-house org.
36. Assaulted
40. Readied, as a range
43. Bear a grudge against
44. Cash holder
46. Slanting
47. Not as firm
48. Manages
49. Exceedingly bad

DOWN

1. Teacher of a sort
2. Snockered
3. Kind of union
4. "Dinotopia" network
5. "Break time!"
6. Poet ___ Wheeler Wilcox
7. Left one's bunk
8. Wood measure
9. More frightening
10. Guides
11. Sanford's British inspiration
13. Furious
16. Subterranean chamber
20. Skirt feature
24. Sugar-rich liquid
25. Norm's wife on "Cheers"
26. Rebukes sharply
27. Add moisture to
28. Really relish
30. Guilty, e.g.
33. Many a Hoot Gibson picture
35. Vexatious people
37. Out
38. End of a Beatles song title
39. Monty Python member Gilliam
41. Word following privately or hand
42. Garry Trudeau's "Check Your ___ at the Door"
45. Runner, of sorts

Answers on page 185.

A Little Bit of Everything

ACROSS

1. Bar tallies
5. Included in an e-mail
9. Middle of a game
12. The rain in Spain
13. River connected to the Tiber by a canal
14. Org. with TKOs
15. Relative of Old Man Winter?
17. "Son of," to a Saudi
18. Something to play for
19. Beast of Borden
21. Pool stick
23. Part of a 3-piece suit
25. News for a gossip columnist
26. Poop deck's place
27. Chef's creations
29. "Lions for Lambs" director
33. Closes back up
34. Dijon dissent
35. Go under
37. Get under the skin of
38. Seventh out of 24, Greek-style
39. Midlife crisis symptom
41. Brother on "Frasier"
43. ___ voce (with one voice)
44. Reels from a punch
48. Homer's neighbor
49. Land measure
50. Cream, for one
51. Bunyan's tool
52. "Star Trek" actor Tim
53. Singer-songwriter Tori

DOWN

1. Muslim's cap
2. Muslim general, especially in Turkey
3. Old firefighting method
4. Samurai's quaff
5. Many a builder
6. Athletic shoes
7. Lowest commissioned rank in U.S. Navy: abbr.
8. Shower fondness
9. Is coercive
10. Angie's role on "Law & Order"
11. "Cave ___!" ("Beware of the dog!")
16. High temperatures
20. Willingly
21. Word after used or touring
22. Visiting alien vessel
24. Climbers for creepers
28. Old Fords
30. Swimmers with toxic blood
31. Deteriorate
32. Chain material
35. Animal wildlife
36. Take over, as territory
40. Nicholas II was the last one
42. "Tell Mama" singer James
45. Old French coin
46. A "Road" picture destination for Bob and Bing
47. Urgent cry for help

Answers on page 186.

Overlaps

ACROSS

1. Caustic substance
4. Movie terrier
8. Nabe
12. Hairy-bodied insect
13. Crockpot creation
14. Extended
15. Chipotle
17. Goes out at the card table, in a way
18. Overlapping sports organization?
20. Kind of button
23. Midwest city whose name means "hospitality"
24. Starring role for John Barrymore
25. Hagar the Horrible's daughter
28. Overlapping books?
34. Jump on the ice
35. Ready for surgery
36. Large antelope
40. Vena cava neighbor
41. Overlapping military base?
45. Goody-goody
46. Where clips are frequently seen
50. Stead
51. Its state fish is the Bonneville Cutthroat trout
52. Pasture sound
53. Lively
54. Columnist Myerson
55. One place to see airplanes

DOWN

1. Fourth after FDR
2. Delegate vote
3. Jellied fish
4. Fish jelly
5. Leave be
6. Jamboree structure
7. GI on the lam
8. Snack for a snail
9. Dominion
10. Bored feeling
11. Not knowing where to turn
16. Story
19. Retreat
20. Ed Norton, to Ralph Kramden
21. Tuna type
22. Danielle Steel's "Message from ___"
25. 16-digit numbering system, for short
26. Rhyming tribute
27. Goalkeeper's ideal score
29. It has a checkered past
30. Portable tune players
31. Calder Memorial Trophy winner in 1967
32. Kind of sales
33. Day ___
36. Pertain
37. "Beavis and Butt-head" spinoff
38. One with a towel
39. Have it out (with)
40. Egyptian crosses
42. Split ticket?
43. Fashionable, in a way
44. Hamlet's lament
47. Seagoing inits.
48. Source of cork
49. Route

Answers on page 186.

Not in the Dairy Case

ACROSS

1. Testing site
4. Absorb, as gravy
9. Cadge
12. ___ Miss
13. Command to a lifter
14. Seek office
15. Variety of squash
17. "This American Life" host ___ Glass
18. Net receipts?
19. Major shipbuilding city
21. "The Happy ___," Harry Connick, Jr., holiday song
23. It may be blonde
24. Cable TV network
27. "…and seven years ___…"
29. Emblem on Canada's flag
33. Candy bar ingredient
37. Bridge
39. "The lowest form of humour": Samuel Johnson
40. Color in Canada's flag
41. Tree used for chair seats
44. Women's article of clothing
46. Temporary window replacement, sometimes
50. Off the cuff
54. Kia subcompact
55. Fountain offering
57. Bollix
58. Take control of
59. AC/DC lead singer ___ Scott
60. Run off at the mouth
61. Classic battle participants
62. Long in the tooth

DOWN

1. Brain region
2. Reunion attendee, briefly
3. Kind of software release
4. Natural plastic
5. Done, to Donne
6. Hunger pain
7. Tongue neighbor
8. Colorful part of a plant
9. Guardhouse
10. Currency adopted by Slovenia in 2007
11. Chew like a beaver
16. Cause of sudden death?
20. Put on the market
22. E-tail?
24. Lecture no-nos
25. Thimbleful
26. Newbery Medal org.
28. Alley ending?
30. Listening device
31. Had some food
32. Gave some food to
34. Felt sure about
35. Baby lion
36. Freeway access points
42. Center of power
43. "Hack" star David
45. Promotions
46. Michael Crichton novel
47. Former currency of Turkey
48. Prince Andrew's dukedom
49. Caen couple
51. University of New Mexico athlete
52. Graven image
53. Rubber or brass follower
56. "Two heads ___ better than one"

Answers on page 186.

Triple Cross

ACROSS

1. Exaggerated sense of masculinity
9. Steady throbbing
13. Beehive
14. Perry battle site
15. Moved in a certain direction
17. Paul Bunyan used one
18. Wedding column word
19. Artifices
20. BMW transmission
22. Wingless insect
25. Sister, perhaps
26. Golden ratio constant
29. Girl with a basket
33. Classic-rock group
34. Dr. Evil's Mr. Bigglesworth
35. Cycle competitor
36. Tend to tots
39. Ring-shape isle
42. Wouk's "The Winds of ___"
43. Yuri Andropov headed it for 15 yrs.
46. Gulf Coast city
49. State of irritation
50. Kind of care
52. Cry in court
53. Movie ticket mandate

DOWN

1. Spy name
2. Spot for the winner of king of the hill
3. Motion picture
4. Suckered
5. Holmes's friend Adler
6. Hit song, usually
7. Place for crib notes?
8. "Walking on Thin Ice" musician
9. Swains
10. Misreckons
11. Staff member
12. Harper of "Tender Mercies"
16. Wicked act
20. Slender swimmer
21. Prim do
22. Wield a wok
23. Jeans maker
24. Bradley and Begley
26. Party person?
27. Move like a bunny
28. Words from the bride and groom
30. Poker words
31. Bit of ointment
32. Boater, for one
36. Gridiron charge
37. Location of the House of the Seven Gables
38. Neighbor of an Armenian
39. "Are not!" rejoinder
40. Theatrical award
41. Theatrical award
43. Bruce Lee role
44. Hoover hiree
45. Cotton quantity
47. Emissions-regulating org.
48. Echolocation user

Answers on page 186.

Q Tips

Use a "Q" in place of the sound "cue" in the answers to a few of these clues.

ACROSS

1. Present opener?
5. Short note
9. Tasseled hat
12. Juicy fruit
13. Julia Jean Mildred Frances Turner's professional name
14. Occupy a certain position
15. Feminine name suffix
16. Spitz-like dog
18. Mathematical procedure?
20. It's charged and ready to go
21. Settled in
25. "Don't ___ Love It"
28. Except that
30. Beginning of a conclusion
31. Attempt to end confinement, perhaps?
35. Star turn at La Scala
36. Scottish surname starter
37. Pueblo hrs.
38. For free
41. Union agreement
43. Chinese medical practice?
48. Charity
51. Send sprawling
52. Accessory for Miss Piggy
53. Rick's old flame in "Casablanca"
54. Boundary line
55. Easter candy shape
56. Coastal flier
57. Diversion

DOWN

1. Gp. that Ecuador left in 1992
2. "I ___ man with seven wives...": 2 wds.
3. Part of NRA
4. Ba'ath Party member, perhaps
5. Batting position
6. Check
7. Make permanent, as a signature
8. Lake in the Sierra Nevada range
9. Wintertime bane
10. One, for a Hamburger
11. A's opposite, in England
17. Military assault
19. Gray wolf
22. Adjust cargo
23. Some stars have big ones
24. Illuminated word on a street corner
25. Rocky outcropping
26. German title
27. Where Brunei is
29. Pro ___ (for now)
32. Land near Bahrain
33. Oscar winner of 1988
34. Bon Scott's band
39. Dramatic announcement
40. Spout used to draw off sap
42. Badger cousin
44. "Back in the ___"
45. Literary language of Pakistan
46. Teamsters' vehicles
47. Blade that "touches"
48. Homer's dad
49. Fireplace insert
50. One way to get a putout

Answers on page 187.

Temperature's Rising

ACROSS

1. Bush and Clinton
5. "No, thanks": 2 wds.
10. Spike, as a drink
14. Late-night host Jay
15. ___ Vader of "Star Wars"
16. Israel's Abba
17. One way to quit: 2 wds.
19. Pita sandwich
20. With all sincerity: 2 wds.
21. Drizzles
22. Old Nissan
23. Wrangler's rope
24. Tidy lottery prize: 2 wds.
29. Licorice-flavored plant
33. Roulette color: Fr.
34. Ballerina Pavlova
35. Dryer-trap content
36. Molten material
37. Echelon
38. Court minutes
39. "Would ___?": 2 wds.
40. Willing and able partner
41. Reception with open arms: 2 wds.
44. Turn edible
45. Song title that means "you are" in Spanish: 2 wds.
50. Diamond side
51. Prelate's title
54. "Yikes!"
55. Showing off
56. Publisher Henry
57. Of interest to Audubon
58. Slight advantage
59. Sets down
60. Office furniture
61. Type of ringer

DOWN

1. Spanish hero: 2 wds.
2. Former hotelier Helmsley
3. Narrow waterway
4. Bubbly drinks
5. Words said with a shrug: sl., 2 wds.
6. Skin
7. Torah storers
8. Editor's "put it back in"
9. Like a shrinking violet
10. Pass laws
11. Ethiopia, formerly
12. Drew "Doonesbury," e.g.
13. Baseball Hall of Famer Slaughter
18. Cease-fire
21. Prefix with function
23. Former coin of Italy
25. Words before fours: 2 wds.
26. Line of thinking
27. Old-style copier
28. Quaint negative
29. "There oughta be ___": 2 wds.
30. Costa Rica neighbor
31. Complex nature
32. Herd panics
36. Bearing
40. Equip anew
42. Freshly painted
43. Subatomic particles
46. Goaded, with "on"
47. Rudely sarcastic
48. Polynesian kingdom
49. Dangled a carrot before
50. Cut down
51. Chess action
52. Elevator man
53. Fargo's state: abbr.
55. Fooled

Answers on page 187.

All Mixed Up

ACROSS

1. Kind of list
5. Pasta topper
10. Fence the goods, say
14. Moonfish
15. Forearm bones
16. Lose brightness
17. Aviator pleads?
19. Forest unit
20. Said it wasn't so
21. Salty septet
23. Terminus
24. Orch. section
26. Bombing on stage
28. "Slammin'" golf legend
32. Prepares clams, perhaps
35. Turkish honorific
36. Music-maker's org.
38. Whom Bugs bugs
39. Hound sound
41. Bush
43. Light tune
44. Offer one's 2 cents
46. "Like a Rock" rocker
48. Museum-funding org.
49. Domingo and others
51. Alcoves
53. Leaves
55. Meter maid leavings: abbr.
56. Massages elicit them
58. A pop
60. Many John Wayne movies
64. Anger, and then some
66. 17-Across, 11-Down, and 30-Down, all mixed up
68. [Sigh]
69. Thrusting weapon
70. Speak with vitriol
71. Flappers' hairdos
72. Urged, with "on"
73. Certain NCOs

DOWN

1. Swamp critter
2. Mayberry kid
3. "Aw, heck!"
4. "Excuse me, waitress?"
5. Summer outfit
6. Priest's robe
7. French articles
8. Like some parrots
9. University application parts
10. Toward the stern
11. Naked urchins?
12. First place?
13. Prepared for driving
18. Insurance giant
22. Location
25. Goldman's partner on Wall Street
27. "Little" Dickens girl
28. Wooden shoe
29. Wide open
30. Leathernecks chat?
31. Risk-taker
33. Free-for-all
34. Puerto Rican misses: abbr.
37. Washington's ___ Sound
40. Fort with a fortune
42. Summoned
45. Buffalo's lake
47. Change the price, maybe
50. Horse home
52. Cool red giants in the sky
54. Scrawny one
56. Swift, compact horse
57. Heavenly overhead?
59. Suspend
61. Online periodical
62. Monthly payment for some
63. Retired jets: abbr.
65. Slalom curve
67. Cooler contents

Answers on page 187.

Menagerie Nursery

ACROSS

1. Skating event
6. Rick's "Casablanca" love
10. Door feature
14. Comedian Murphy
15. Former Georgia senator
16. College in New Rochelle
17. It's below the knee: 2 wds.
19. Lara Croft raids it
20. Short joke: hyph.
21. Knockout drink
23. Hot under the collar
24. City on the Po River
26. Was in session
27. Thankless one
31. The Pips, to Gladys Knight
35. Hits the roof: 2 wds.
36. Utah's Hatch
37. Little boy
38. Youth with a lamp
41. Suitability
43. Iceberg alternative
44. Swedish flier
45. Palindromic vehicle
47. Melville captain
51. Seaport of Italia
54. Phone call opener: 2 wds.
56. Citizens' rights group: abbr.
57. Revolver maker: 2 wds.
59. It smooths things over
60. German auto
61. March honoree, familiarly: abbr., 2 wds.
62. Off-color
63. Part in a play
64. Actor Davis

DOWN

1. River to the Rio Grande
2. Hersey's "A Bell for ___"
3. Time waster
4. Biathlon weapon
5. Prefix with "sweet"
6. Newspaper pullouts
7. Monetary gain
8. Weekend TV fare: abbr.
9. Flower or swimmer
10. Scout of the Old West: 2 wds.
11. Secluded spot
12. Round-buyer's words: 2 wds.
13. Diaper wearer
18. Take the lid off
22. Swallows
25. Prefix with place or print
26. Old timer
28. Composer Thomas
29. Cash register section
30. Ice cream brand
31. Sow's mate
32. Alice's Restaurant patron
33. Overcrowd
34. Engage in horseplay: 2 wds.
39. Tooth for gnawing
40. Name divider
41. In general: 3 wds.
42. French capital, in song
46. Water-conserving critter
47. Bank units: abbr.
48. Gym game
49. Ike's opponent
50. Actress Davis
51. Execute perfectly, slangily
52. Approx. 4,047 square meters
53. Clear snow-covered roads
55. Furthermore
58. GI mail drop

Answers on page 187.

Picket Line

ACROSS
1. Creole veggie
5. Spread seed
10. Strategy
14. Hyena's hideaway
15. $100 bill
16. Lounge (around)
17. Arrest at an English school?
19. Wistful word
20. Avoid
21. Catch in a trap
22. Fed. retirement agency
23. Grumbles
25. Snake charmer's pet
29. Book after Micah
31. Like a short play
33. Stephen of "V for Vendetta"
34. Sailor's greeting
38. Sarandon and Sontag after a fight?
41. Collection of computer bits
42. Legal matter
43. Before the deadline
44. "Then again, I could be wrong"
46. Track athlete
47. Tex-Mex treats
51. Splashy resort
53. Eyeball-bending paintings
54. Guess-the-murderer story
59. Lawn additive
60. Picket line at Shea Stadium?
62. ___ instant
63. When repeated, a word of solace
64. Annoys
65. Lascivious look
66. Dad's sisters
67. Makes known

DOWN
1. Designer Cassini
2. Winslet of "Finding Neverland"
3. Run amok
4. Pisa's river
5. Macbeth and Duncan, e.g.
6. To be returned
7. Kind of whistle
8. JFK posting
9. Austrian article
10. Drawing-board original
11. Bochco legal drama
12. Arkansas's ___ Mountains
13. Flunkies' responses
18. John of "Being John Malkovich"
21. Addition solution
23. Tool building
24. Kind of
25. Ty or Lee J.
26. Nothing but
27. Ready to hit the hay
28. Marathon, for one
30. Playground retort
32. ___ cotta
34. Home of some bubbly
35. Precipitation pellets
36. Treater's words
37. River to the North Sea
39. Wants
40. Like a messy bed
44. Famed ballplayer Mel
45. Souvenir shop item
47. Manuscript leaf
48. Mimic's forte
49. Actor Malcolm- ___ Warner
50. Ryan of "The Beverly Hillbillies"
52. Proverbial pig containers
54. Architect with an avian name
55. Banned submachine guns
56. Nick's partner
57. Like a Parker?
58. Lass in a Hardy tale
60. RR terminal
61. Wed. follower

Answers on page 188.

Face the Music

ACROSS

1. Herr von Bismarck
5. Skin doctor's field: abbr.
9. Aptly named fruit
14. "If I may be so bold…"
15. Neighborhood
16. Girl rescued by Don Juan
17. He wrote what was originally called "Defense of Fort M'Henry" in 1814
20. 1968 hit with the lyric "I like the way you walk, I like the way you talk"
21. Prepares text for publication
22. Split pea, e.g.
24. Private address?
25. Econ. yardstick
28. Feed holder
30. Large sea ducks
35. 1964 Oscar-winning actress Kedrova
37. Deep grooves
39. Earth's path
40. "More optimistically…"
43. Sheer curtain fabric
44. Red Cross supplies
45. Slow flow
46. Make beloved
48. Seldom seen
50. "The Spanish Tragedy" dramatist
51. Pro's opposite
53. International org. since 1881
55. Floral ornaments
60. Down Under denizen
64. Seismology tool
66. Kid's song refrain
67. Place in order
68. RAM unit
69. Philosopher Kierkegaard
70. WWW addresses
71. Miss Trueheart, of old comics

DOWN

1. Clumsy sorts
2. Drive-___ window
3. Afternoon socials
4. Bygone Dodge models
5. Iced rum cocktail
6. Hospital trauma centers: abbr.
7. Nap, maybe
8. "Miracle on 34th Street" store
9. Like some motives
10. Obtains
11. Cotton to
12. "Okay if ___ myself out?": 2 wds.
13. What Simon does, in a kids' game
18. Industry big shots: abbr.
19. Early Ron Howard role
23. Outlet inserts
25. Hand protector
26. Smooth, sheer fabric
27. Kilt's pattern, often
29. Miscellaneous category
31. First 007 movie
32. Online library offering
33. Snazzy
34. Spirited mount
36. Competent
38. Wander off the path
41. Stimulus response
42. Sets aside (for)
47. Campus military org.
49. Old 5-franc pieces
52. Associate of Gandhi
54. Fancy tie
55. AAA travel recommendations

56. The Buckeye State
57. Crystal ball studier
58. New York canal

59. Headliner
61. Rational
62. Spots in the Seine

63. Mouse-sighting shrieks
65. Photo blow-up: abbr.

1	2	3	4	■	5	6	7	8	■	9	10	11	12	13
14				■	15				■	16				
17			18					19						
20					■	21								
■	■		22			23	■	24			■	■	■	■
25	26	27	■	28			29	■	30		31	32	33	34
35			36	■	37			38	■	39				
40				41					42					
43					■	44				■	45			
46				47	■	48			49	■	50			
■	■	■	51			52	■	53			54		■	■
55	56	57	58			59	■	60			61	62	63
64						65								
66				■	67				■	68				
69				■	70				■	71				

Answers on page 188.

Things Are Heating Up

ACROSS
1. Pottery class gunk
4. Drain the energy from
7. Actresses Evans and Hamilton
13. Opp. of WSW
14. President's time in office
16. Tiny critter seen on a slide
17. U.S. spy org.
18. Nobel winner Harold who discovered heavy hydrogen
19. Suggested indirectly
20. Little consolation
23. Summer in Paris
24. Clownish action
25. Western Hemisphere org.
26. Mo. after Mar.
28. One who stays calm during a tense situation
33. Game with Professor Plum
36. "___ to Joy"
37. Common way to fortify table salt
38. Fled
39. Chant sounds
40. Hockey great Bobby
41. Org. that sticks to its guns

42. Pay what is owed
44. Bullring cheer
45. Walrus relative
46. Not be a first-string player
49. "___ about time!"
50. ___ ___ glance
51. Partner of aahed
55. Unit of electrical resistance
57. Passionate
60. Realm
62. Prefix for logy or gram
63. First U.S. st.
64. ___ ___ ___ million
65. CNN offering
66. Pitcher's stat.
67. Turn the color of a beet
68. Queue after Q
69. Happy for glad: abbr.

DOWN
1. Holy city of Islam
2. Teamsters, e.g.
3. Did a poker task
4. Wall plaster
5. Early plane prefix
6. Casts a shape in advance
7. Cowardly Lion portrayer Bert
8. One who mimics
9. "Smoking or ___?"

10. Decide conclusively
11. Help in a crime
12. Marquis de ___
15. "Get outta ___ ___!" ("Stop hassling me!")
21. Craps cubes
22. Big Ten sch.
27. Pea holder
29. Energy or enthusiasm
30. Ambulance wail
31. Poet Pound
32. Actual
33. Gullet
34. Actress Turner
35. Like some beards or Christmas trees
39. Do better than
40. Shrub also known as a rose bay
43. Paramedic: abbr.
44. Get
45. Loafer, e.g.
47. Dine
48. Kelly to Regis
52. Lord of the underworld
53. Each
54. Raspy singer Bob
55. Smell
56. Sharpen, as a knife
58. Put ___ ___ act (pretend)
59. Mountain drinks?
61. Help

Answers on page 188.

Treetops

ACROSS

1. Gossip
4. Self-righteous person
8. ___ jure (by the law itself)
12. Hurry-scurry
13. Heckelphone cousin
14. Housekeeper
15. Body of lawyers
16. Colonial pattern of hospitality
18. Flightless bird
20. Certain bead makeup
21. Leader with no responsibilities
25. Resistance to change
26. Safecrackers
30. Uplifting attire
31. Shoot down
33. Sénat vote?
34. Montenegro dwellers
37. Frog variety
40. Popular name for a home-repair product
42. Sudden attack
44. Drivel
45. Rubbery candy
48. Maryland's state tree
51. "My Girl" star Chlumsky
52. It may be a penny
53. Yonder yacht
54. Peel off
55. June 6, 1944
56. Graffiti signature

DOWN

1. Quick punch
2. Oklahoma headquarters of the Chickasaw Nation
3. Drive in the form of a screw
4. Roy Lichtenstein's genre
5. What you get for driving someone home: abbr.
6. Former Romanian president Iliescu
7. Amelia and Abigail Gabble in "The Aristocats"
8. Prevent
9. He got a brand new bag, in song
10. Reservoir deposit
11. Poetic tribute
17. Not toward
19. Dickens's "___ Mutual Friend"
21. Misinformation pieces
22. Concerning
23. Teutonic article
24. First name in Rastafarian movement
27. One of four on a football field
28. Mentor
29. Competing team
32. Gen ___
35. Nickname giver on ESPN
36. Dispatch
38. Large bird of prey
39. European Tour grp.
41. Substitute for "mea culpa"
42. Grand ___ Railroad
43. Dodge car
45. Subject of Boyle's law
46. Stop running
47. "One Day ___ Time" (TV series)
49. Epiphany exclamation
50. Beer container

Answers on page 188.

As You Will

ACROSS

1. Summer getaway
5. Choke off a cry
8. Sail supports
13. Khayyám
14. Elephant boy of the movies
15. Former USSR cooperative
16. It might be for better or worse: 3 wds.
18. Meadow overpass
19. Rivals at war
20. Marked
22. Levin and Gershwin
23. "I get ___ out of you...": 2 wds.
24. Appear to do well
27. Estop, in law
30. Boston watchword: abbr.
31. Actress Eleonora, et al
33. Photo tone
34. Diamond or Young
36. Jumping sticks
38. Atmospheric pollution
39. Dais principal
41. Mountains of Utah
43. Summer quaff
44. Wrestling maneuver: 2 wds.
46. Thinker, in a way
48. "The bald ___" (Dogpatch denizen)
49. Opposed, in 48-Across locale
50. Tests for better results
52. Milksops
56. Foreclose on ___: 2 wds.
57. Be encouraged: 2 wds.
59. Cohered
60. Flock members
61. Line a roof
62. Etta's cartoon relatives
63. Type of alert
64. A dish for José

DOWN

1. Where coos are heard
2. "___ for All Seasons": 2 wds.
3. Manufacture
4. Early newborn, for short
5. Electromagnetic unit
6. Cut short: abbr.
7. Icelandic poet who wrote in Danish
8. Gummy substances
9. Items
10. Mugger, of a kind: 2 wds.
11. Scope or photo start
12. Kane's Rosebud
14. Become misty: 2 wds.
17. Ventilated
21. Greek or Turkish weight
24. Pulitzer poet: 1929
25. Swelling
26. Stand pat: 3 wds.
27. Schoolyard game, ___ the ring: 2 wds.
28. Vacuum tube
29. Excited
32. Tar's gear
35. Opposing generals or actress's full name: 2 wds.
37. Smokes
40. Ruchings, e.g.
42. Foolishly imitative
45. Grand ___ Opry
47. Katydid, for one
49. Questioned
50. Pool hall equipment
51. She: Fr.
53. UN-related group centered in Vienna: abbr.
54. Novelist Ambler
55. Town on the Vire: 2 wds.
58. Overwhelm

Answers on page 189.

Manly Names

ACROSS

1. Dodge traffic, perhaps
8. Narrow estuary
13. Momentum
14. Good-bye, maybe
15. South American hero
16. Three-masted ship
17. "Monday Night Football" network
18. Old stereo component
20. Classroom sights
22. Pennington and Cobb
23. Cambodian currency
24. Vieira's cohost
26. Boot base
27. Befitting a blackguard
31. Paella ingredient
32. One member of Houston's NFL team
33. Bird with a snood
34. Foot, to Flavius
35. Leia strangled him
39. Small, as a town
42. Like many basketball players
43. Devonshire dad
44. A number that designates place
46. Patronized a certain restaurant
47. State of perfect inner peace
48. Finds peace
49. Scanner dial

DOWN

1. Sudden shift while sailing
2. Narrow winning margin
3. Short shouts
4. Dermal features
5. Off-road ride: abbr.
6. Bloody Mary's daughter
7. Mr. Miyagi's gift to Daniel
8. Documents sent by phone
9. "___ Three Lives"
10. Actor Paul in the College Football Hall of Fame
11. Jennifer Lopez movie
12. High-stepping horse
19. Corning glass
21. ___ Marino
25. Speak
26. Having healing powers
27. At an acceptable level
28. Recent delivery
29. Oogenesis products
30. Capt.'s superior
34. Where cables connect
36. Uninspiring
37. Maillot ___ (Tour de France jersey for younger competitors)
38. Sufism deity
40. Preliminary race
41. "Coming to America" actor La Salle
45. ___ Hill (music group)

Answers on page 189.

All for Naught

ACROSS

1. Fixes
7. Tanks and such
12. Good places for basking
14. Gina's good
15. Swish shot
17. Mancinetti opera "___ e Leandro"
18. Turns sharply
19. Work on roots, perhaps
20. Parisian tenant's payment
22. Harder to grasp
24. Texas shrub
27. Grasslands
28. Post office request
31. Off-white
32. Preminger and von Bismarck
33. Walking
35. Stares
39. Big initials in old films
40. Enterprise communications officer
43. Phone menu no.
44. Harsh policy
47. Space shuttle part
48. Play during the day
49. Rejoinder in a kids' argument
50. "Grease" high school

DOWN

1. "Lou Grant" star
2. Poet Marianne
3. John with a piano
4. Slangy dissent
5. Kind of window
6. Trigonometry function
7. Maltreatment
8. Monotonous practice
9. French exclamation
10. Like many leases
11. Olympic judges
13. Actuarial datum
16. Chicken piece
21. Universal donor
23. Peruvian novelist Mario Vargas ___
25. Mythical thread-spinner
26. Soundstage cry
28. Screaming Yellow ___
29. Facing severe punishment
30. History teacher in the "Luann" comic strip
31. Russian wolfhound
34. Expenses
36. Pasta with diagonally cut ends
37. Win laurels
38. Sharpening device
41. German city on the Danube
42. Adjective in a Hitchcock title
45. "Season of Glass" singer
46. Legal follower

Answers on page 189.

Grammar School

ACROSS

1. "Buona ___ " (Italian greeting)"
5. Some are green
9. Recidivate
14. Valhalla VIP
15. Ill-considered
16. Homeric tale
17. The real McCoy?
20. Deficiency of red blood cells
21. Soothing stuff
22. Barbie's beau
23. Obsolete Pakistani currency
25. Ready
27. Lizard, old style
30. Baker's dozen?
32. Someone who raves
36. Anchor
38. Vault
40. Effectively cut short
41. Third from last
44. Epitome
45. General Sherman is a huge one
46. Breezed through
47. ___ Day, August 1
49. Ball material
51. "Don't give up!"
52. Mark left by Zorro?
54. Barber's job
56. Can. neighbor
59. Diva's delivery
61. Points on a map with equal barometric pressure
65. To badly speak of one?
68. Glue
69. Was philanthropic
70. Kind of wire
71. Was available for stud
72. Smeltery input
73. "What are the ___ ?"

DOWN

1. Scotch's partner
2. Biblical plot
3. Abounding
4. The inner self (Jung)
5. Percussion instrument
6. "Dig in!"
7. In the Red?
8. Characteristic of a mudstone
9. The learned
10. Foreman's superior
11. Basketball maneuver
12. Ad headline
13. Heaven on Earth
18. Opening time, maybe
19. Guffaw
24. 007?
26. Bottom line in medical treatment?
27. Spam container
28. Henry, Jane, or Peter
29. Emblematic pole
31. Long-beaked fish of temperate Atlantic waters
33. Piece of land
34. Organic compound
35. Long and slender
37. Large quantity of written matter
39. Plicate
42. Mollified
43. Earthenware casserole dishes
48. Hindu wrap
50. Not final or absolute
53. Beatle
55. Guiding principle
56. Independent federal agency for mail processing and delivery: inits.
57. Run-in
58. To boot
60. Winston Churchill's "___ Country"
62. Shuttlecock
63. All fired up
64. Gym set
66. Four-time Japanese prime minister
67. "___ Got a Secret"

Answers on page 189.

Mail Service

ACROSS

1. Achieve through deception
8. Native Israeli
13. "Told you so"
14. Really dug
15. Chump
16. Smiling
17. ___ Conner, Miss USA 2006
18. Seemed likely
20. Tonto's horse
22. Wade opponent
23. Emergency med. procedure
24. Sings the praises of
26. Obligation
27. Business address, perhaps
31. Parliamentary procedures?
32. Hubbub
33. KITT or General Lee
34. New Deal monogram
35. Emulated a sous chef
39. Tree carvings
42. Malcolm Arnold's "Fantasy for Cello," for example
43. Fabrications
44. Best possible
46. Latin clarifier
47. Childlike attitude
48. Gives off, as light
49. Met at the door

DOWN

1. Partner of figures
2. Violinist Stern
3. Part of TNT
4. Attacks
5. Disparity
6. Tale-teller
7. "American History X" star
8. Noncom's nickname
9. Plugging away
10. Den denizen
11. Approach quickly
12. Bird in "B.C."
19. Polite refusal
21. Chinese ideal
25. Norwegian "ouch"
26. Putting down
27. Promoting peace
28. National anthem since 1980
29. Three make a turkey
30. Potential bait-taker
34. Bruce Lee's weapons
36. Doomsday cause, perhaps
37. Fill with happiness
38. Handed (out)
40. Experiment
41. Category of crystals
45. Casual Friday omission

Answers on page 190.

Another Pangram

In this crossword puzzle, every letter of the alphabet is used at least once.

ACROSS

1. Soul food ingredient
8. Gets a pot going
13. Professional lightbulb producers?
14. Climb aboard
15. Greek wine
16. Pulmonary valve neighbor
17. Location of the highest known mountain in the solar system
18. Source of a couch potato's potatoes?
20. Poles, e.g.
22. Greg Bear novel
23. Tina Fey's old show, for short
24. Retort to "You are not!"
26. Governmental appointee
27. Heap
30. Bar with coconut
32. ___ acetate
33. Type of scheme
35. Compression skill
36. Wall Street figure, for short
37. Batter before Casey
41. 1994 Best Picture nominee
44. Travel guide listings
45. Worrier's woe, they say
46. Heather has two, in a kids' book
48. Make rhapsodic
49. Dots on some signage
50. Popular appetizer
51. Medium-size combos

DOWN

1. Companies
2. "Let's Make ___"
3. Popular aquarium fish
4. It takes a big bow
5. Actress Dolenz
6. Unit of change
7. Varlets
8. With masts fully extended
9. Where both hands are up?
10. Hits the sack
11. Bien ___ (of course)
12. Hollywood comer
19. Lollapalooza
21. Xylem fluid
25. Biblical resin
26. Competition restriction, perhaps
27. Canada explorer Cartier
28. Ecclesiastical vessel
29. Rhapsodic
31. State Dept. figure
34. Fusion weapons
36. Comparable to a beet?
38. Doting
39. Showed reverence, maybe
40. Curves in the road
42. Zeus starter
43. Got threadbare
47. Agent 86

Answers on page 190.

In Other Words

The answers to a few of these clues can be found by scrambling the words in the clues themselves.

ACROSS

1. Literary collection
4. Ruin's partner
9. Rebuke
13. Decrease
15. Consumed
16. A little, in music
17. Greedy
18. Got up
19. Type of chamber
20. Notarial cheater, in other words: 2 wds.
23. Overjoy
24. Final
25. Free
28. Listens to
33. Sweep's foe
37. Ruler on the Rialto
40. Actor Davis
41. Mutilate scepter, in other words: 2 wds.
44. Marie Antoinette, e.g.
45. Jannings or Ludwig
46. Tibetan oxen
47. Plus
48. Pinch
50. Koufax stats: abbr.
54. Odor
59. Braille primrose, in other words: 2 wds.
65. Country on the Caspian
66. Like some skirts
67. Dross
68. Average: hyph.
69. Growing out
70. Bingo kin
71. Mound builders
72. Stymie
73. NYSE purchase: abbr.

DOWN

1. Cognizant
2. Of the seagoing service
3. Loos or O'Day
4. End of dependence
5. ___ avis: Lat.
6. Semicircular island
7. Jai alai equipment
8. On hands and ___
9. Risky investment: abbr.
10. Arm of a firth
11. Feel every muscle
12. Down and out
14. Emend
21. Above: poet.
22. One of 3 swordsmen
26. Mt. ___, Crete
27. Love lavishly
29. Spot
30. On the main
31. Casablanca nightclub owner
32. Complete outfits
33. Koran section
34. Cheers for Ferdinand
35. "Miss ___ Regrets"
36. Prong
38. Precious stone
39. Land of loughs
42. Foot, for Frost
43. Actor Wallach
49. Anderson or Tillis
51. Stormed
52. Favorite Garbo word
53. Jack of rhyme
55. Take a chance
56. Famous Canadian physician
57. Signified
58. Peloponnesian city
59. Mona ___
60. ___ horse
61. Phloem
62. Grandson of the first family
63. Network
64. Baltic feeder

Answers on page 190.

Presidential Portraits

ACROSS
1. Yawn-inducing
5. Wren or hen
9. Mushroom-cloud maker
14. College in New Rochelle
15. Buffalo's lake
16. Palmer, to pals
17. Collette of "In Her Shoes"
18. Zip
19. Championship
20. First jug at the bar?
23. Failures, in slang
24. Small pooch, briefly
25. Polyester brand
28. Nicholas or Peter
30. Stylish, once
33. Online sales
34. Opportunities for repentance
35. Granada greeting
36. Suffix with Congo
37. Great grade
38. Group of soldiers
39. "The Wizard of Oz" actor
40. One of the Brady Bunch
41. Tylenol alternative
42. Football's Parseghian
43. Methods
44. Took part in the game
45. "Say no more!"
47. Goes out with
48. Storage of angling gear?
55. Ward off
56. Per unit
57. Couple, in a column
58. Joiner's phrase
59. Julia of "The Addams Family"
60. Forum home
61. City on the Ruhr
62. Prime the poker pot
63. High-tech suffix

DOWN
1. They may be boring
2. Rifle
3. Visitor to Siam
4. Source of hot air
5. Harmless
6. Fairway choices
7. One year in a trunk
8. Heartfelt
9. Carroll's mad tea drinker
10. Building unit
11. Where to see presidential portraits?
12. Denver's elevation, roughly
13. Brewski
21. Screwdriver, e.g.
22. "No, thanks"
25. Perry's secretary
26. On ___ (rampaging)
27. The ability to sing and play guitar, to Johnny?
28. Scrabble pieces
29. Cozy
31. Kind of drab
32. Passé
34. Full of pep
35. Island attire
37. Yawning
41. Obi-Wan player
43. Chinese dumpling
44. Tune from "Funny Girl"
46. Pang
47. Pub potable
48. Celebrity
49. Currier's partner
50. Fictional Georgia plantation
51. Bridge
52. Part of Ripley's phrase
53. Nautilus commander
54. Feds

Answers on page 190.

Mister Ed-ucation

ACROSS

1. Admit
6. Reverse or neutral
10. Norwegian metropolis
14. From Rome: prefix
15. Crucifix inscription
16. Atop of
17. Take it off
18. Rivers of comedy
19. Price displayers
20. Cuties that lack depth?
22. Garfield's sidekick
23. Raw metal
24. Trick shot in a film, e.g.
26. Visit briefly
30. Emphatic turndown
32. Duct drop
33. Sky sightings
35. Horizontal line on a graph
39. K-12, textbook-wise
40. Kind of tournament
42. Storied captain
43. Cap attachment
45. New Age music superstar
46. Nibble, beaver style
47. Weather, in a way
49. Wishful thinking
51. Boardroom echoes
54. "Diamonds ___ Forever"
55. Keen on
56. Mister Ed-ucation?
63. Alt.
64. Part of a Faulkner title
65. Online letters
66. Superman's lady
67. Model airplane builder's need
68. Capone colleague
69. Fashion's Christian
70. Sentry's cry
71. Elders and alders

DOWN

1. Talk like Daffy Duck
2. Place in a Robert Redford movie
3. Canvas covering
4. Former netman Nastase
5. "Piece of cake"
6. Toy soldier
7. Chemical compound
8. Uzbekistan border sea
9. Salon jobs
10. Where to take the roast?
11. Bogart sleuth
12. Mr. Spock's strong suit
13. Advent
21. Wither
25. Tricky situation
26. Remarriage prefix
27. Fabled archer
28. Surfer's paradise
29. Top van driver?
30. Everybody's opposite
31. Anthem opening
34. Ricky's landlord
36. "___ : Warrior Princess"
37. Mosque VIP
38. Pen mothers
41. Bebé holder
44. Poet's before
48. In the heavens
50. Mind terribly
51. Give up
52. Communist leader Zhou ___
53. Kind of pad or pool
54. Up to the present
57. Earthenware jar
58. Julia of Hollywood
59. Bahrain biggie
60. Corddry of "Studio 60 on the Sunset Strip"
61. Building location
62. Tigers foe

Answers on page 191.

Dense Design

ACROSS

1. Not clerical
5. "Jacques ___ is Alive and Well…"
9. Magnetic flux symbol
12. Lhasa ___
13. Name used by some Roman emperors
15. Sleep over
17. Wildlife lover of TV fame
18. USN officer
19. Set up tents
23. Become attached
27. Yellow stick
28. Parlor order
31. Choir nook
32. Some "old maids"
33. Found out
36. Short smoke
37. Expurgate
42. 1984 George Burns sequel
45. "___ Class" (sitcom)
46. Head lines, for short?
47. Summer clock setting: abbr.
48. Counter offer
49. Where bulls and bears run: abbr.

DOWN

1. Dundee damsel
2. Dr. meeting
3. What the Latin "video" means
4. What most TVs will require in 2009
5. Opaque fabric
6. European coal area
7. "Maid of Athens, ___ part": Byron
8. Kerensky's successor
9. Chinese calendar animal
10. "I don't get it"
11. Ideal ending
14. Merry Men's color
16. Supergiant in Cygnus
20. Soothing ingredient
21. Lunch or brunch
22. Some fishing traps
23. Saltwater lake
24. Survive
25. Mafia thing
26. "I'm scared!"
29. Eremite
30. Cooked a chimichanga, e.g.
34. Tissue masses
35. Theatrical Tharp
38. Honeybunch
39. World Series of Poker regular Phil
40. Turns on a jagged course
41. Something ___
42. Off the wall
43. Time pieces: abbr.
44. Understand

Answers on page 191.

Watch What You Say

ACROSS

1. Didn't take part, with "out"
6. The Crimson Tide, to fans
10. Misses
14. "Keen!"
15. Old Glory, for one
16. Not fantastic
17. Stop with
18. She gets what she wants
19. Queens's ___ Stadium
20. Old married folks?
22. Do, say
23. Null service
24. "Cut that out!"
26. Iron output
30. Court activity
32. Director Kazan
33. Quiz answer
35. Finds fault
39. Pickled delicacies
40. Stable dads
42. Page
43. Where the mouth is
45. Musical finale
46. Certain something
47. Cupid's dart
49. Fossil preserver
51. "___ Kate"
54. Diana Ross musical, with "The"
55. Type of history
56. They watch what you say
63. Painter Magritte
64. Peace Nobelist Wiesel
65. On the up and up
66. Fork over, with "up"
67. Ship of Columbus
68. ___ Gay (WWII plane)
69. Tide type
70. Furniture wood
71. Thing of value

DOWN

1. Your
2. Confined
3. "There!"
4. Series ender
5. "Go on!"
6. Black key on a piano
7. Gobs
8. Kind of bonding
9. Tennis great Andre
10. Tavern for health nuts?
11. Fable fellow
12. "Chicago Hope" actress Christine
13. Slushy stuff
21. Track events
25. Center X or O
26. Herbicide target
27. Protected from the wind
28. All you can eat
29. Like a quick somnambulist?
30. "Presumed Innocent" author Scott
31. English horn, for one
34. "Little Caesar" gangster
36. Enlist again
37. Start for scope or meter
38. Petty quarrel
41. Composer Erik
44. Hurler's asset
48. Ease up
50. Showy shrub
51. Islam's sacred text
52. Castle of many steps
53. Rooftop visitor
54. Unleash
57. "Would ___ to you?"
58. Colada fruit
59. Retreats
60. Some stars have big ones
61. Stir up, without a spoon
62. RBI, for one

Answers on page 191.

Triple Stackers

ACROSS
1. Theme song for "Rocky III"
14. Change accounts
15. Anxiety over a purchase
16. Psychologist LeShan
17. One-tenth of a percent of a cool mil
18. Gets in the game
19. Start illegally
21. Move like goo
24. It's left of center?
25. Slightest bit of money
28. Dead ringers
32. Track
33. Elton's john
34. Quadrant borders
35. Surgeon's instrument
38. Bathroom fixture
41. Run up the phone bill
42. Patrol car broadcast
45. Quarter back?
48. Part of the FBI?
49. Watch words?

DOWN
1. Kathryn of "Law & Order: Criminal Intent"
2. "___ be surprised"
3. Actor Baskin of "Air Force One"
4. Ring shout
5. Skip
6. Where rasters form
7. "Good grief!"
8. "Maid of Athens, ___ we part"
9. Small primate
10. ___ fell swoop
11. Encircled
12. Enya sometimes sings in it
13. Explorer John and actress Charlotte
19. Wise (to)
20. Distinct style of beer: abbr.
21. Unorthodox
22. Reset setting
23. Stationary demographic concept: abbr.
25. Reason for an NC-17 rating
26. Magnetite or hematite
27. Battleship letters
29. Aristocracy, e.g.
30. Cyberspace snicker
31. Longish fish
35. "Wittgenstein" director Jarman
36. Letter after Sierra
37. West Indian sorcery
38. Court payment
39. Mae West's "___ Angel"
40. Band with the 1980 hit album "Freedom of Choice"
42. Lookin' to fight
43. Tread tediously
44. Affleck and Stein
46. Windy City train initials
47. Words before crossroads

Answers on page 191.

A Little California

ACROSS

1. Walk between cars, perhaps
8. Verbal digs
13. Anxious
14. Provide the wherewithal
15. Aztec language
16. Suddenly run (at)
17. Has the stage
18. Wind moniker
20. Smelly smoke
22. Home of some mil. pilots
23. Put a dent in
24. Alphabet ender
26. City on the Seward Peninsula
27. Like some tension
30. Failed in the clutch
32. Secretary of War Alphonso whose son later held the position
33. Venomous snake
35. Time period
36. Ringgit subdivision
37. Deacon Jones was one
41. Island whose name is Spanish for pelican
44. Hill of "Psych"
45. Actress Lenya
46. Leg bones
48. Porterhouse kin
49. Where to find Getz's girl
50. Early Judean king
51. Symbols used by coaches during chalk talks

DOWN

1. Contemporary of Cass and Jimi
2. As ___ resort (when all else fails): 2 wds.
3. Company founded by Jerry Yang and David Filo
4. Exhausted
5. Bloc for a doc
6. "Why don't we!"
7. Frequent duettist with Tony Bennett
8. Passenger safety items
9. Blue hue
10. Go nuts
11. Major star
12. Pierced
19. Spingarn Medal awarder: abbr.
21. 1950s singer Sumac
25. Young eel
26. "Saturday Night Live" regular, 1985–90
27. Cat burglar's need
28. Ring site
29. Unknown element
31. Daughter of Loki, in Scandinavian myth
34. Stuck, in a way
36. Bucephalus, for one
38. Decreed
39. Site to remember
40. Monument Valley sights
42. ___ cost
43. Speeds
47. Pasture sound

Answers on page 192.

6 × 13

ACROSS

1. Tracy/Hepburn classic
9. Singer Lane
13. Ersatz meat products
15. Freckle-faced magazine mascot
16. ___ Fail, Ireland's coronation stone
17. Cambodian statesman Lon ___
18. Talk show host, to fans
19. 21 spots
21. Broadway's first Tevye
24. Fish with electroreceptors
25. Minuscule
28. Haircut style
32. Curtail speech
33. Shoe classification
34. 1:10, e.g.
35. Arctic herd
38. Words of parting
41. Get a blue ribbon
42. Skip on water
45. Being developed
48. Like many stump speeches
49. Defeats a bridge contract
50. Yesteryear

DOWN

1. Of grandparents
2. Bagel depot
3. Belgian filmmaker
4. Corp. boss
5. Cathedral city S. of Florence
6. Makeovers
7. Response to an offer
8. Frank wrapper
9. Chills
10. "Let It ___" (song)
11. Use rodomontade
12. Thrall of yore
14. Take another turn in Trivial Pursuit
19. Jailer's charge
20. Teachers union, for short
21. Fam. planning goal
22. MLB stat
23. Prepare for yachting
25. Rolled dough?
26. Where to get in line?
27. Aliens
29. Went under
30. Profit ender?
31. Indebtedness initials
35. Harry and Roy
36. Two-legged rifle support
37. A fourth of a gal.
38. Smoky treats, briefly
39. Apropos of
40. The Galactic Empire's "Imperial Walker"
42. Per ___
43. One of the Stuarts
44. Motel restrictees
46. Devout, to Da Vinci
47. Him, in Le Havre

Answers on page 192.

Frequent Flier

ACROSS

1. Chess win
5. Oodles
10. Does sums
14. Aid in crime
15. Playwright Edward
16. Robert Frost work, e.g.
17. Printed matter
18. Tribute with friendly insults
19. Preminger or Klemperer
20. Severe shocks
22. When fewer people are online, e.g.
24. Surgery sites: abbr.
25. Sluggishness
27. What a polygraph test may reveal
28. Furnish food
30. What trick-or-treaters push
32. ___-jerk reaction
33. "My Big Fat Greek Wedding" actress Vardalos
34. Suffix with profit or racket
35. Frequent flier?
41. Response to "Are you?"
42. Owl's cry
43. Is unable to
44. Spot
48. Caterpillar or grub
49. Fuss and bother
50. Get really close
52. German article
53. Minuteman's enemy
55. A con artist pulls this
57. Tickled-pink feeling
58. They make trumpets less loud
60. Grandson of Adam
61. Pipe elbows
62. Wipe away
63. Thompson of "The Remains of the Day"
64. Take a load off
65. Groups that broke away
66. Bird abode

DOWN

1. Digging tools similar to pickaxes
2. Different from normal behavior
3. Oil, in "The Ballad of Jed Clampett"
4. "___, Brute?"
5. Plastic wrap brand
6. Neared, with "on"
7. Lawyers' grp.
8. Spaniard who explored the Mississippi
9. Ignite
10. Each, in pricing
11. "This I gotta hear!"
12. Minor point
13. Prepares ham
21. Former Russian orbiter
23. Name on a pencil
26. Driver who won't let you pass
29. Causing goosebumps
31. Kane of "All My Children"
33. Get specific about people
36. Final word
37. Folk music gathering, e.g.
38. "So sorry"
39. Makes poisonous
40. Eyes rudely
44. ___-than-life
45. "Let's Eat Right to Keep Fit" author Davis
46. Sings in the Alps, perhaps
47. Junction with surgeon's stitches
48. Bandleader Brown
51. Operates with a beam
54. "___ la vie"
56. Last year's 12-year-old
59. Tic-___-toe

Answers on page 192.

The Hard Stuff

ACROSS

1. Mosquito or fly
5. Hula skirt material
10. Swelled heads
14. Something to think about
15. Crimean seaport
16. Have too little
17. Venomous snake
19. Fashion magazine
20. Combining form meaning "in front"
21. By means of
23. Alley- ___ (basketball play)
24. Grinch creator
25. Sharp mind, figuratively: 2 wds.
28. Imbibe daintily
29. Inventor Howe
31. Actress Ryan
32. Stewpot: Sp.
34. Belief system
35. Tall president, for short
36. It's a sure thing: 3 wds.
41. Dorm VIPs
42. Summer hours in NYC
43. Site for a bell
45. For this purpose only: Lat., 2 wds.
48. Chord type
50. Li'l Abner's Daisy ___
51. Old name for a locomotive: 2 wds.
53. Arab leaders
55. Neighbor of Israel: abbr.
56. Suffix with diction
57. Response to a naysayer: 3 wds.
58. "Schindler's List" star Neeson
60. Billionaire's girlfriend, maybe: 2 wds.
63. Behold to Brutus
64. Licorice-flavored plant
65. Give the old heave-ho to
66. Gone out with
67. Hornets' homes
68. Decides on, with "for"

DOWN

1. Painter Pablo
2. Al Bundy on "Married … with Children": 2 wds.
3. Consisting of seven parts
4. Saves for later viewing
5. Greek sandwich
6. Stadium noise
7. Pub offering
8. Forestalls, with "off"
9. Dogpatch denizen Hawkins
10. Meadow mama
11. Aplenty
12. To be returned: 2 wds.
13. Treeless tract
18. Celtic language
22. Suspect's story
25. Spanish ayes
26. Interferes, as with evidence
27. General drift
30. "My ___ are sealed"
33. Composer Copland
35. Court records
37. Cottage for Putin
38. Actress Falco
39. Arising: 2 wds.
40. Most raspy
44. Vacation spots
45. Nuptial paths
46. Frozen carbon dioxide: 2 wds.
47. Mann of education
48. "Taste this": 2 wds.
49. Metric prefix
52. Kind of transplant
54. Myopic cartoon character
57. Fateful day
59. Word on a door
61. Fleur-de- ___
62. "Spring ahead" syst.

Answers on page 192.

Answers

Zoo Story (page 4)

Breakfast's Ready (page 8)

Lip Service (page 6)

Let's Get Away from It All (page 10)

For the Birds (page 12)

```
A C R I D   B E E P   S P A M
R H I N O   A L V A   T A C O
T A L K T U R K E Y   O R T O
E R E   E N D S   S T O K E D
      E L I S   O U R L A D Y
C O B A L T   L A P U P
A L E G   A S I S   E I G H T
R E A L   S T E E L   G U A M
R O M E O   R O S A   E L L E
      S A L O N   U S O P E N
O L D C H A P   E R I N
P O R O U S   A L E X   E T A
E S A U   E A T I N G C R O W
R E N T   R A T A   U S A I R
A R K S   S A Y S   N A S T Y
```

Wax On, Wax Off (page 16)

```
S S T S   N A P S   P H I
O K R A   O M I T   E I N
M O O N S H I N E   S A T
M A L A W I   K E T T L E
E L L   E T C   P A L E R
      A L T A R   P E A S
A P P L E P O L I S H
D R O P   R E A I R
A M P L E   D D T   M R I
P O L Y P S   S H O O I N
P I A   I N T H E B U F F
E R R   C I A O   I S L E
R E S   S T O W   S E E R
```

Profit in Baskets (page 14)

```
V I S E   D I S H   G A B
O C H S   O R E O   U N E
D E E P S L E E P   I N D
K I D N A P   M E A N E R
A N S   W H E E   B E T E
      O F I D   Y E A T S
N O T H I N G B U T N E T
O N E A T   A L P S
N L E R   P R E P   C A D
S E N A T E   A I E L L O
K A I   E A S T E R E G G
I V E   A C R E   M A A M
D E R   R E I D   A R E A
```

A Matter of Time (page 18)

```
W A I T E   T S P   O A F
A N N E X   E P A   H M O
S T A M P   S A S S I E R
    S P L I T S E C O N D
S I T S O N   M O O
C S A   I C Y   R O A M
U P T O T H E M I N U T E
D Y E R   W O N   T V S
      A A A   T H R A S H
T W E L F T H H O U R
W E B S I T E   U R G E S
O N A   R A W   S A U T E
S T Y   E R S   E L E C T
```

Patriotic Songs (page 20)

Explore Your Mind (page 24)

Echoes (page 22)

Autumn Delight (page 26)

Fit to Be Tied (page 28)

It's Magic (page 32)

Help by Another Name (page 30)

Use Some Sense (page 34)

'70s Fads (page 36)

I	M	A	C		T	L	C		C	P	A	S
L	A	R	A		A	A	A		O	A	H	U
E	X	A	M		I	M	P	E	L	L	E	D
	B	E	L	L	B	O	T	T	O	M	S	
		R	A	F		S	E	E	M			
C	B	R	A	D	I	O			R	I	S	E
A	Y	E		S	N	O	R	E		N	I	L
M	E	S	A		P	E	T	R	O	C	K	
	P	E	T	E		I	T	A				
L	E	I	S	U	R	E	S	U	I	T		
A	C	R	O	B	A	T	S		S	A	V	E
P	R	E	P		S	O	U		I	K	E	A
D	U	D	S		E	N	E		N	E	X	T

Records (page 38)

R	I	A	S		I	D	E	A	S		A	W	A	Y
I	T	C	H		M	I	S	D	O		S	R	T	A
P	U	T	O	N	P	A	P	E	R		S	I	L	L
S	P	I	R	A	L	L	Y		T	O	A	T	E	E
		A	M	O	S		C	E	N	S	E			
L	I	M	N	E	D		C	A	R	E	S	S	E	R
O	D	E		D	E	C	A	L		S	I	D	L	E
L	I	M	O		D	A	R	E	S		N	O	L	I
L	O	O	P	S		K	E	B	A	B		W	I	N
S	T	R	E	A	M	E	D		C	R	A	N	E	S
		A	N	N	A	S		C	R	A	M			
P	A	N	N	E	D		S	H	I	V	E	R	E	D
R	O	D	E		M	A	K	E	S	A	N	O	T	E
O	N	U	S		A	L	I	S	T		D	U	N	E
D	E	M	S		N	A	S	T	Y		S	T	A	R

Crossing Caution (page 40)

C	A	L	F		R	A	V	I		R	A	B	B	I
A	B	E	L		I	R	A	N		U	N	L	I	T
T	U	N	A		G	I	M	P		S	I	E	N	A
S	T	O	P	T	H	E	P	R	E	S	S	E	S	
			J	U	T	S		I	V	I	E	D		
C	A	M	A	R	O		A	V	I	A		W	P	A
A	M	O	C	O		H	E	A	T		S	H	O	R
L	O	O	K	W	H	O	S	T	A	L	K	I	N	G
I	N	N	S		A	L	O	E		O	U	T	D	O
F	G	S		P	R	E	P		M	O	L	E	S	T
			H	A	I	T	I		T	A	S	K		
	L	I	S	T	E	N	T	O	R	E	A	S	O	N
S	O	N	A	R		O	H	N	O		W	A	K	E
S	T	E	N	O		N	A	T	O		A	T	R	A
S	T	R	A	W		E	T	O	N		Y	E	A	R

Hurry! (page 42)

S	T	A	B		A	L	P		S	L	E	W
O	H	I	O		L	E	E		N	A	P	E
D	O	N	T	W	A	I	T		A	K	I	N
A	U	T	H	O	R		A	S	P	E	C	T
			O	M	E	L	E	T				
G	U	A	R	D	E	D		C	O	H	O	S
U	G	L	I		D	I	M		I	O	W	A
T	H	I	G	H		C	O	A	T	I	N	G
			H	E	C	T	I	C				
B	I	S	T	R	O		S	T	A	T	U	S
E	D	E	N		L	E	T	S	R	O	L	L
T	O	R	O		A	G	E		E	D	N	A
S	L	A	W		S	O	N		A	D	A	M

"Easy" Does It (page 44)

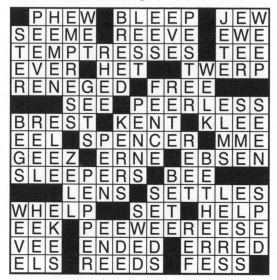

	P	H	E	W		B	L	E	E	P		J	E	W
S	E	E	M	E		R	E	E	V	E		E	W	E
T	E	M	P	T	R	E	S	S	E	S		T	E	E
E	V	E	R		H	E	T			T	W	E	R	P
R	E	N	E	G	E	D		F	R	E	E			
			S	E	E		P	E	E	R	L	E	S	S
B	R	E	S	T		K	E	N	T		K	L	E	E
E	E	L		S	P	E	N	C	E	R		M	M	E
G	E	E	Z		E	R	N	E		E	B	S	E	N
S	L	E	E	P	E	R	S		B	E	E			
			L	E	N	S		S	E	T	T	L	E	S
W	H	E	L	P		S	E	T		H	E	L	P	
E	E	K		P	E	E	W	E	E	R	E	E	S	E
V	E	E		E	N	D	E	D		E	R	R	E	D
E	L	S		R	E	E	D	S		F	E	S	S	

Dairy Folk (page 48)

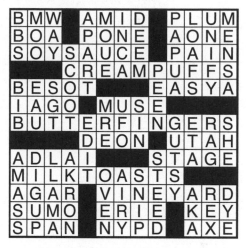

B	M	W		A	M	I	D		P	L	U	M
B	O	A		P	O	N	E		A	O	N	E
S	O	Y	S	A	U	C	E		P	A	I	N
			C	R	E	A	M	P	U	F	F	S
B	E	S	O	T				E	A	S	Y	A
I	A	G	O		M	U	S	E				
B	U	T	T	E	R	F	I	N	G	E	R	S
			D	E	O	N			U	T	A	H
A	D	L	A	I			S	T	A	G	E	
M	I	L	K	T	O	A	S	T	S			
A	G	A	R		V	I	N	E	Y	A	R	D
S	U	M	O		E	R	I	E		K	E	Y
S	P	A	N		N	Y	P	D		A	X	E

Summertime Fun (page 46)

C	E	D	E		A	Y	E		L	A	S	S
B	A	I	L		L	A	P		E	L	I	A
S	U	N	S	H	I	N	E		M	E	N	U
		G	E	E		K	E	R	O	U	A	C
T	A	B		R	U	E		U	N	T	I	E
S	L	A	V		S	E	P	I	A			
P	E	T	A	L	S		E	N	D	E	A	R
		C	O	R	E	R		E	X	P	O	
A	M	M	A	N		A	U	G		P	E	T
B	O	O	T	E	E	S		A	O	L		
A	C	T	I		S	E	A	S	H	O	R	E
S	H	O	O		A	L	B		O	R	A	L
E	A	R	N		U	S	E		H	E	N	S

Venomous (page 50)

B	I	B		T	A	B		O	A	T	E	R
U	S	A		A	L	A		N	U	R	S	E
L	A	N		J	E	L	L	Y	F	I	S	H
B	A	J	A		X	B	O	X		V	E	E
S	C	O	R	P	I	O	N		G	I	N	A
			R	O	S	A		T	R	A	C	T
S	A	R	I	S			M	U	L	E	S	
P	R	O	V	E		S	C	A	N			
E	A	S	E		S	T	I	N	G	R	A	Y
A	B	A		S	O	A	R		E	A	V	E
K	I	N	G	C	O	B	R	A		B	A	N
T	A	N	Y	A		L	U	G		B	I	T
O	N	E	P	M		E	S	E		I	L	L

Bad Weather (page 52)

U	S	E		N	Y	P	D		V	I	N	E
P	U	G		O	A	H	U		I	R	O	N
L	I	G	H	T	N	I	N	G	B	O	L	T
A	T	T	A	C	K			E	R	N	I	E
T	O	O	T	H		A	S	S	A	Y	E	R
E	R	S			A	M	U	S	T			
	S	T	O	R	M	D	O	O	R			
		I	O	T	A	S				E	S	P
S	A	G	E	H	E	N		F	A	C	T	O
O	S	S	I	E			T	A	I	L	O	R
T	H	U	N	D	E	R	S	T	R	U	C	K
T	O	I	T		M	E	A	T		S	K	Y
O	T	T	O		S	P	R	Y		E	S	S

Pitching Records (page 56)

H	A	L		T	O	X	I	N		J	A	W
O	U	I		A	L	E	R	T		E	G	O
O	R	E	L	H	E	R	S	H	I	S	E	R
R	O	D	E	O	S			B	U	N	K	
A	R	O	S	E		R	E	S	I	S	T	S
Y	A	W			N	E	R	T	Z			
	N	O	L	A	N	R	Y	A	N			
		N	I	N	E	S				E	T	C
C	A	T	S	P	A	W		T	A	M	I	L
O	B	I	E				G	E	N	E	V	A
W	A	L	T	E	R	J	O	H	N	S	O	N
E	T	E		L	E	A	V	E		I	L	K
R	E	D		F	O	R	T	E		S	I	S

Get a Move On (page 54)

T	O	O	T		E	C	H	O		S	E	D	A	N
E	A	V	E		C	H	U	M		L	L	A	N	O
C	H	E	R		R	O	L	E		O	I	L	E	D
H	U	R	R	Y	U	P	A	N	D	W	A	I	T	
	C	A	R				S	O	P					
A	S	A		S	T	O	A		C	O	M	B	A	T
S	T	L	O		O	R	C	A		K	E	E	N	E
F	O	L	L	O	W	T	H	E	L	E	A	D	E	R
A	P	E	A	R		S	E	R	E		T	W	A	S
R	E	D	F	I	N		S	O	T	S		A	R	E
			G	O	O				A	P	R			
	B	E	H	I	N	D	T	H	E	T	I	M	E	S
O	L	E	A	N		E	R	A	S		N	E	R	O
D	E	L	T	A		T	I	L	T		T	R	A	Y
E	D	S	E	L		S	O	L	E		A	S	T	A

Horsing Around (page 58)

T	H	A	I		C	U	B	A		I	B	M
A	U	L	D		A	P	E	D		M	O	I
P	R	E	E	M	P	T	E	D		P	I	N
	L	E	A	V	E	O	N	E	C	O	L	T
			S	P	F			D	H	S		
E	A	R			E	C	S	T	A	T	I	C
T	H	E	R	O	A	D	T	O	R	O	A	N
C	A	R	E	F	R	E	E			R	M	N
		O	A	F			A	P	B			
A	L	U	M	I	N	U	M	F	O	A	L	
J	O	T		C	A	L	I	C	O	C	A	T
A	V	E		I	T	E	N		Z	E	R	O
R	E	D		O	L	E	G		E	S	S	E

Deli Misadventures (page 60)

R	H	O		A	R	C	H		T	A	D	A
A	O	L		B	U	R	Y		A	N	E	W
I	W	A	S	I	N	A	P	I	C	K	L	E
D	E	F	O	G		B	E	R	T	H	E	D
		B	A	A		S	K	I				
Y	O	U		I	L	E		L	O	U	D	
A	W	F	U	L	L	Y	C	H	E	E	S	Y
P	E	O	N		E	R	A		R	A	E	
		B	I	D		Y	S	L				
E	L	B	O	W	E	D		S	E	A	R	S
F	U	L	L	O	F	B	A	L	O	N	E	Y
T	R	O	T		A	L	O	E		T	A	N
S	E	W	S		T	S	K	S		I	R	E

Fencing Off (page 64)

G	O	O		A	B	I	T		V	E	A	L
A	L	F		N	A	D	A		I	P	S	E
G	E	T	A	G	R	I	P		B	E	T	A
			L	U	N	G	E	B	R	E	A	K
W	A	S	P	S			D	O	A			
A	C	E			S	W	E	A	T	B	E	E
T	H	R	U	S	T	A	C	C	O	U	N	T
T	E	A	M	W	O	R	K			D	D	T
			B	A	R			B	O	S	S	A
P	A	R	R	Y	M	A	S	O	N			
A	Q	U	A		I	C	E	W	A	T	E	R
R	U	N	G		N	E	A	T		A	V	E
K	I	T	E		G	Y	R	O		S	E	X

Have Some Moore (page 62)

M	R	S		S	T	A	R		A	W	E	S
A	B	E		K	U	D	U		C	E	N	T
L	I	V	E	A	N	D	L	E	T	D	I	E
		E	T	T	A		E	V	I	G	A	N
M	I	N	C	E		O	D	E		E	C	O
A	N	T	E		I	R	O	N	S			
A	S	H	T	O	N	K	U	T	C	H	E	R
			C	U	T	I	T		R	A	G	E
A	T	A		T	E	N		V	E	N	O	M
R	A	T	E	D	R		T	I	E	D		
T	H	E	L	O	N	E	R	A	N	G	E	R
S	O	I	L		E	V	I	L		U	F	O
Y	E	N	S		D	A	B	S		N	F	C

Balancing Act (page 66)

A	J	A	R		L	O	C	O		S	A	D
S	I	L	O		A	V	O	N		U	N	E
P	L	O	W		T	E	S	T	S	I	T	E
	T	E	E	T	E	R	T	O	T	T	E	R
			D	E	R		S	P	E	C		
A	S	S		R	O	E			E	A	T	S
R	O	C	K	I	N	G	H	O	R	S	E	S
F	L	U	E			G	A	L		E	X	T
		L	E	N	S		P	E	G			
T	I	P	P	I	N	G	P	O	I	N	T	
S	A	T	S	C	O	R	E		Z	E	A	L
A	G	E		E	R	I	N		M	E	M	O
R	O	D		R	E	P	S		O	D	E	S

Sew You Say (page 68)

Z	E	E		M	I	L	E		J	E	E	P
E	A	T		O	N	Y	X		E	R	A	T
U	R	N		N	A	R	C		L	I	R	A
S	P	A	C	E	N	E	E	D	L	E		
			L	Y	E		R	A	Y			
O	H	I	O			V	P	S		R	B	I
H	A	N	G	B	Y	A	T	H	R	E	A	D
O	W	N		M	E	N			A	F	R	O
			A	W	L		T	S	P			
		T	E	S	T	P	A	T	T	E	R	N
P	A	I	R		S	A	N	A		W	O	E
J	O	N	I		I	N	K	Y		O	U	I
S	K	Y	E		N	E	S	S		K	E	N

Winter Wonders (page 72)

W	A	S		O	H	M	S		L	O	A	M
A	N	T		R	E	A	P		E	L	S	E
S	N	O	W	B	A	L	L	F	I	G	H	T
P	A	P	A		D	E	A	R		A	Y	E
			H	A	W		T	I	P			
A	L	A		G	A	S		G	A	F	F	E
H	O	C	K	E	Y	P	L	A	Y	E	R	S
S	T	E	E	L		Y	E	T		D	O	T
			G	E	M		O	E	R			
E	T	A		S	O	A	P		A	U	N	T
C	H	R	I	S	T	M	A	S	T	R	E	E
R	O	I	L		T	Y	R	O		G	S	A
U	R	A	L		O	L	D	S		E	S	S

Films of 1941 (page 70)

A	C	H		W	H	A	M	O		A	D	O
P	R	E		H	A	R	E	M		L	I	B
P	E	N	N	Y	S	E	R	E	N	A	D	E
L	A	C	E				G	I	S	T	S	
E	K	E	O	U	T		H	A	N	K	I	E
			N	I	C	E		J	A	M		
	C	I	T	I	Z	E	N	K	A	N	E	
	A	C	E		Z	E	R	O				
T	R	E	N	D	Y		I	S	O	B	A	R
O	F	F	E	R				W	I	R	E	
M	A	L	T	E	S	E	F	A	L	C	O	N
B	R	O		C	U	P	I	D		E	M	T
S	E	E		K	E	A	T	S		P	A	S

International Headlines (page 74)

	P	A	D	S		C	H	I	C		P	H	A	T
	O	B	I	T		R	O	N	A		L	O	C	O
	T	H	E	I	R	I	S	H	S	T	E	W	E	D
A	P	O		R	E	S		E	S	O	B	E	S	O
S	I	R	S		T	I	A	R	A	S				
K	E	S	E	Y		S	T	E	N		S	O	L	E
			L	O	S		A	N	D		C	A	I	N
T	H	E	D	U	T	C	H	T	R	E	A	T	E	D
A	E	R	O		A	H	A		A	L	L			
G	R	A	M		G	E	L	T		L	E	E	C	H
				P	E	Y	T	O	N			D	A	R	E
P	A	L	E	A	L	E		P	S	A		S	E	X
T	H	E	F	R	E	N	C	H	F	R	I	E	D	
A	S	S	T		F	N	M	A		A	R	L	O	
S	O	T	S		T	E	A	T		B	A	S	S	

Treed (page 76)

Comic Hero to Movie Star (page 78)

Funny Guys (page 80)

Cover Up (page 82)

Fruit Salad (page 84)

```
J O A N ■ A M A S S ■ I T E M
E L B A ■ B A S I C ■ N O R A
A D A M S A P P L E ■ S P I N
N I S E I ■ ■ S O N ■ O B E Y
S E E R E S S ■ ■ S E L M A ■
■ ■ ■ S N O O P ■ S O N N E T
S A L ■ A A R O N ■ P I A N O
I L E D ■ P E N A L ■ A N O N
M A M A S ■ S C O O P ■ A L E
P R O M P T ■ E M A I L ■ ■ ■
■ N O A H S ■ I M P A S S E
T A L C ■ E L I ■ ■ E V E N S
E L A L ■ L U N C H D A T E S
L O W E ■ M S D O S ■ B O L A
L E S S ■ A H O O T ■ O N L Y
```

About Face (page 88)

```
P L A N ■ B L A D E ■ S P A R
I A G O ■ A A R O N ■ L A N A
T H E T U R N I N G P O I N T
A R R A N G E D ■ ■ A G R E E
■ ■ ■ ■ T I E S ■ F O R A ■ ■
H A B I T S ■ D E M A N D S ■
O M O O ■ ■ O I L E D ■ R I A
P O I N T O F N O R E T U R N
I R S ■ E A T E N ■ ■ A P E S
■ S E D A T E D ■ M A S A D A
■ ■ ■ A S S N ■ B E L T ■ ■ ■
S T A R E ■ ■ S E R P E N T S
T U R N S O N T H E S T E A M
A N T E ■ A R E A L ■ H A R E
R E E L ■ F A N N Y ■ E R N E
```

Colorful Clues (page 86)

```
W O E ■ D R E W ■ S P O T
H U T ■ O A T H ■ H O P E
I C H ■ Z I T I ■ R O U X
P H O N E N U M B E R S ■
■ ■ L O N ■ ■ P A W ■ ■ ■
Y E O W ■ A X E L ■ K I A
E X G I R L F R I E N D S
S T Y ■ E L L S ■ L E S S
■ ■ G E O ■ ■ O L E ■ ■ ■
■ U S E D C A R V A L U E
W R E N ■ A M I E ■ I V Y
I S T O ■ T E N N ■ N E E
N A S A ■ E N D S ■ G A S
```

Start of Something Big (page 90)

```
O V E N ■ A B C S ■ O O H
T E X T ■ D R A T ■ A V E
I T C H ■ V I C E ■ H A R
S O U ■ L I G H T B U L B
■ ■ S K I S ■ E S E ■ ■ ■
I D E A T E S ■ S P C A
N U M B E R O N E S E E D
S H E A ■ ■ W I D E N E D
■ ■ L E A ■ T A S K ■ ■ ■
W H E A T G E R M ■ N I X
A A A ■ H O R A ■ Z I N E
V H S ■ A N A T ■ A F R O
Y A Y ■ N Y S E ■ P E E N
```

If You Want to Get Technical (page 92)

B	U	T		O	N	C	E		J	A	W	S
A	T	E		R	A	I	L		A	S	A	P
Y	A	M		L	I	T	E		P	O	N	Y
	H	P	L	O	V	E	C	R	A	F	T	
		U	N	E		T	E	N				
Z	E	S	T		E	R	A		V	I	A	
A	M	A	Z	O	N	W	A	R	R	I	O	R
P	U	P		P	O	E		O	I	N	K	
		S	I	S		P	G	A				
	G	A	T	E	W	A	Y	A	R	C	H	
T	A	C	O		E	C	R	U		O	A	R
E	V	E	R		A	M	E	N		W	H	O
D	E	S	K		T	E	X	T		L	A	D

Merry Christmas (page 96)

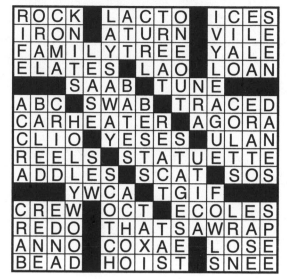

R	O	C	K		L	A	C	T	O		I	C	E	S
I	R	O	N		A	T	U	R	N		V	I	L	E
F	A	M	I	L	Y	T	R	E	E		Y	A	L	E
E	L	A	T	E	S		L	A	O		L	O	A	N
		S	A	A	B		T	U	N	E				
A	B	C		S	W	A	B		T	R	A	C	E	D
C	A	R	H	E	A	T	E	R		A	G	O	R	A
C	L	I	O		Y	E	S	E	S		U	L	A	N
R	E	E	L	S		S	T	A	T	U	E	T	T	E
A	D	D	L	E	S		S	C	A	T		S	O	S
			Y	W	C	A		T	G	I	F			
C	R	E	W		O	C	T		E	C	O	L	E	S
R	E	D	O		T	H	A	T	S	A	W	R	A	P
A	N	N	O		C	O	X	A	E		L	O	S	E
B	E	A	D		H	O	I	S	T		S	N	E	E

Playing Post Office (page 94)

C	A	S	K		A	U	R	I	C		D	O	O	M
A	L	L	Y		P	L	A	T	A		U	G	L	I
F	O	U	R	L	E	T	T	E	R	W	O	R	D	S
E	E	R	I	E		A	M	A	H		E	S	T	
			E	G	G	S		S	T	E	P			
R	P	M		O	O	H	S		S	E	R	E	N	E
E	R	I	C		T	O	P	S		Z	O	N	E	D
P	U	S	H	T	H	E	E	N	V	E	L	O	P	E
A	D	O	R	E		S	L	O	E		E	L	A	N
Y	E	S	I	A	M		L	O	I	S		A	L	S
			S	C	O	W		P	L	E	A			
I	S	M		U	R	A	L		A	M	A	S	S	
S	T	A	M	P	O	F	A	P	P	R	O	V	A	L
L	U	G	E		S	E	N	O	R		N	E	R	O
E	D	I	T		E	R	A	S	E		G	R	I	P

Carrying On (page 98)

P	E	A	L		G	R	A	S		C	A	R	V	E
U	R	S	A		O	U	S	E		A	L	I	E	N
B	A	S	K	E	T	B	A	L	L	G	A	M	E	S
			E	N	C	L		F	I	E				
G	S	A		T	H	E	W	H	O		S	A	Y	A
Y	E	L	L		A	S	H	E	N		E	M	E	R
M	A	B	E	L		E	L	E	V	E	N	A	M	
	B	A	G	P	I	P	E	P	L	A	Y	E	R	
F	I	N	A	N	C	E	D		N	O	S	E	S	
E	R	I	C		E	N	L	A	I		U	T	N	E
D	D	A	Y		M	T	E	T	N	A		Y	D	S
			L	E	A		O	D	D	S				
P	U	R	S	I	N	G	O	N	E	S	L	I	P	S
T	R	I	O	S		O	W	E	N		U	T	A	H
A	N	G	S	T		N	E	S	T		G	O	R	Y

Awfully Nice (page 100)

Animal House (page 104)

Panagram (page 102)

The International Scene (page 106)

Sevens (page 108)

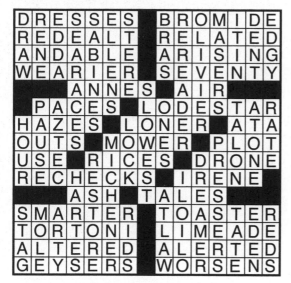

```
DRESSES█BROMIDE
REDEALT█RELATED
ANDABLE█ARISING
WEARIER█SEVENTY
███ANNES█AIR███
█PACES█LODESTAR
HAZES█LONER█ATA
OUTS█MOWER█PLOT
USE█RICES█DRONE
RECHECKS█IRENE█
███ASH█TALES███
SMARTER█TOASTER
TORTONI█LIMEADE
ALTERED█ALERTED
GEYSERS█WORSENS
```

Famous Fare (page 112)

```
SLOW█PIPE█MACES
CUBE█ADEN█ELENA
ONEA█LEND█SOLON
RAYROMANOCHEESE
ERS█MEL██HESS██
███BAR█APES█TWA
OFTEN█ACRE█SIAM
MARTINSHORTCAKE
ICES█AHEM█HOLES
TEA█ABED█CUT███
██TRIO██SAM█SAT
JAMESBROWNBETTY
AREAL█OPEN█COOP
MINCE█WADE█HONE
BATHS█SLED█ODES
```

Gram's Birthday (page 110)

```
LAVA█SOUSA█AGED
ODES█AURAS█DRAY
CENTIGRAMS█RARE
INTONE█LOI█IMPS
███USN█ASSAM███
REGISTER█TENACE
HARTE█PAGET█RON
ERAS█MACED█PINT
ATM█DOLES█MEADE
SOONER█STRAINER
███PELTS█EER███
HAHA█INA█VIANDS
ODOR█CARDIOGRAM
DINE█ERIAS█RASE
STER█SEDGE█ASHE
```

Studio 54 (page 114)

```
ROTATE██ACHES
AIRBALL█ROAST
BLACKLICORICE
BED█EAVESDROP
IDEST█ILE█IRT
███LENDL█VETO
SHRINE█AVERSE
NYET█CORER███
ADV█PTA█RANAT
PREHEATED█OWE
SALESREGISTER
ATILT█ROCKIER
TENDS██STINKY
```

A Little Bit of Everything (page 116)

```
T A B S   C C E D   T A C
A G U A   A R N O   W B A
J A C K F R O S T   I B N
    K E E P S   E L S I E
C U E   V E S T   I T E M
A F T   E N T R E E S
R O B E R T R E D F O R D
    R E S E A L S   N O N
F A I L   R I L E   E T A
A N G S T   N I L E S
U N A   S E E S S T A R S
N E D   A C R E   T R I O
A X E   R U S S   A M O S
```

Not in the Dairy Case (page 120)

```
L A B   S O P U P   B E G
O L E   H E A V E   R U N
B U T T E R N U T   I R A
E M A I L   G L A S G O W
    E L F   A L E
U S A   A G O   L E A F
M I L K C H O C O L A T E
S P A N   P U N   R E D
    E L M   B R A
P L Y W O O D   A D L I B
R I O   C R E A M S O D A
E R R   U S U R P   B O N
Y A K   S E X E S   O L D
```

Overlaps (page 118)

```
L Y E   A S T A   A R E A
B E E   S T E W   L E N T
J A L A P E N O   G I N S
    L I T T L E L E A G U E
P A N I C   X E N I A
A H A B   H O N I
L I M I T E D I T I O N S
    A X E L   P R E P
A D D A X   A O R T A
P A R R I S L A N D
P R I G   T A L K S H O W
L I E U   U T A H   M A A
Y A R E   B E S S   S K Y
```

Triple Cross (page 122)

```
M A C H I S M O   B E A T
A P I A R I A N   E R I E
T E N D E D T O W A R D S
A X E   N E E   R U S E S
    G E A R B O X
F L E A   N U N   P H I
R E D R I D I N G H O O D
Y E S   C A T   A L P O
    B A B Y S I T
A T O L L   W A R   K G B
M O B I L E A L A B A M A
S N I T   P R E N A T A L
O Y E Z   A D M I T O N E
```

Q Tips (page 124)

All Mixed Up (page 128)

Temperature's Rising (page 126)

Menagerie Nursery (page 130)

Picket Line (page 132)

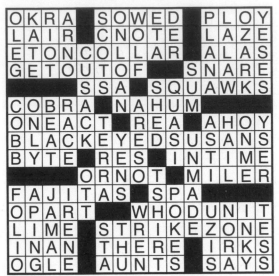

```
OKRA_SOWED_PLOY
LAIR_CNOTE_LAZE
ETONCOLLAR_ALAS
GETOUTOF__SNARE
__SSA_SQUAWKS__
COBRA_NAHUM____
ONEACT_REA_AHOY
BLACKEYEDSUSANS
BYTE_RES_INTIME
__ORNOT_MILER__
FAJITAS_SPA____
OPART__WHODUNIT
LIME_STRIKEZONE
INAN_THERE_IRKS
OGLE_AUNTS_SAYS
```

Things Are Heating Up (page 136)

```
MUD_SAP_LINDAS
ENE_TERM_AMOEBA
CIA_UREY_HINTED
COLDCOMFORT_ETE
ANTIC_OAS_APR
_COOLCUSTOMER
CLUE_ODE_IODIZE
RAN_OMS_ORR_NRA
ANTEUP_OLE_SEAL
WARMTHEBENCH
_ITS_ATA_OOHED
OHM_HOTANDHEAVY
DOMAIN_IDEO_DEL
ONEINA_NEWS_ERA
REDDEN_RST_SYN
```

Face the Music (page 134)

```
OTTO_DERM_UGLIS
AHEM_AREA_LEILA
FRANCISSCOTTKEY
SUSIEQ_TYPESETS
__SOUP_SIR__
GNP_SILO_EIDERS
LILA_RUTS_ORBIT
ONABRIGHTERNOTE
VOILE_SERA_OOZE
ENDEAR_RARE_KYD
__CON_YMCA__
ROSETTES_AUSSIE
THERICHTERSCALE
EIEIO_RANK_ONEK
SOREN_URLS_TESS
```

Treetops (page 138)

```
JAW_PRIG_IPSO
ADO_OBOE_MAID
BAR_PINEAPPLE
_MOA_SWEAT
FIGUREHEAD
INERTIA_YEGGS
BRA_NIX_OUI
SERBS_LEOPARD
_ELMERSGLUE
FORAY_PAP
GUMMYBEAR_OAK
ANNA_ANTE_SHE
SKIN_DDAY_TAG
```

As You Will (page 140)

C	A	M	P	■	■	G	A	G	■	M	A	S	T	S
O	M	A	R	■	S	A	B	U	■	A	R	T	E	L
T	A	K	E	A	T	U	R	N	■	S	T	I	L	E
E	N	E	M	I	E	S	■	■	N	O	T	I	C	E	D
■	■	■	I	R	A	S	■	A	K	I	C	K	■	■
B	E	S	E	E	M	■	P	R	E	C	L	U	D	E
E	D	T	■	■	D	U	S	E	S	■	S	E	P	I	A
N	E	I	L	■	P	O	G	O	S	■	S	M	O	G
E	M	C	E	E	■	U	I	N	T	A	■	A	D	E
T	A	K	E	D	O	W	N	■	O	P	I	N	E	R
■	■	■	I	G	G	L	E	■	A	G	I	N	■	■
R	E	T	R	I	E	S	■	S	I	S	S	I	E	S
A	L	O	A	N	■	T	A	K	E	H	E	A	R	T
C	L	U	N	G	■	E	W	E	S	■	C	E	I	L
K	E	T	T	S	■	R	E	D	■	■	T	A	C	O

Manly Names (page 142)

J	A	Y	W	A	L	K	■	F	I	R	T	H
I	N	E	R	T	I	A	■	A	L	O	H	A
B	O	L	I	V	A	R	■	X	E	B	E	C
E	S	P	N	■	T	A	P	E	D	E	C	K
D	E	S	K	S	■	T	Y	S	■	S	E	N
■	■	■	L	A	U	E	R	■	S	O	L	E
U	N	G	E	N	T	L	E	M	A	N	L	Y
P	E	A	S	■	T	E	X	A	N	■	■	■
T	O	M	■	P	E	S	■	J	A	B	B	A
O	N	E	H	O	R	S	E	■	T	A	L	L
P	A	T	E	R	■	■	O	R	D	I	N	A	L
A	T	E	A	T	■	N	I	R	V	A	N	A
R	E	S	T	S	■	S	Q	U	E	L	C	H

All for Naught (page 144)

A	M	E	N	D	S	■	■	A	R	M	O	R
S	O	L	A	R	I	A	■	B	U	O	N	A
N	O	T	H	I	N	G	B	U	T	N	E	T
E	R	O	■	V	E	E	R	S	■	D	Y	E
R	E	N	T	E	■	■	E	E	L	I	E	R
■	■	■	Y	U	C	C	A	■	L	E	A	S
■	Z	I	P	P	L	U	S	F	O	U	R	■
B	O	N	E	■	O	T	T	O	S	■	■	■
O	N	F	O	O	T	■	■	G	A	P	E	S
R	K	O	■	U	H	U	R	A	■	E	X	T
Z	E	R	O	T	O	L	E	R	A	N	C	E
O	R	I	N	G	■	M	A	T	I	N	E	E
I	S	T	O	O	■	■	R	Y	D	E	L	L

Grammar School (page 146)

S	E	R	A	■	T	E	A	S	■	L	A	P	S	E
O	D	I	N	■	R	A	S	H	■	I	L	I	A	D
D	E	F	I	N	I	T	E	A	R	T	I	C	L	E
A	N	E	M	I	A	■	■	A	L	O	E	■	K	E	N
■	■	■	A	N	N	A	■	Y	A	R	E	■	■	■
E	F	T	■	E	G	G	S	■	R	A	N	T	E	R
M	O	O	R	■	L	E	A	P	■	T	E	R	S	E
A	N	T	E	P	E	N	U	L	T	I	M	A	T	E
I	D	E	A	L	■	T	R	E	E	■	A	C	E	D
L	A	M	M	A	S	■	Y	A	R	N	■	T	R	Y
■	■	■	S	C	A	R	■	T	R	I	M	■	■	■
U	S	A	■	A	R	I	A	■	I	S	O	B	A	R
S	P	L	I	T	I	N	F	I	N	I	T	I	V	E
P	A	S	T	E	■	G	A	V	E	■	T	R	I	P
S	T	O	O	D	■	O	R	E	S	■	O	D	D	S

Mail Service (page 148)

F	I	N	A	G	L	E		S	A	B	R	A
A	S	I	S	A	I	D		A	T	E	U	P
C	A	T	S	P	A	W		R	I	A	N	T
T	A	R	A		R	A	N	G	T	R	U	E
S	C	O	U	T		R	O	E		C	P	R
			L	A	U	D	S		D	U	T	Y
P	O	S	T	O	F	F	I	C	E	B	O	X
A	C	T	S		F	U	R	O	R			
C	A	R		F	D	R		D	I	C	E	D
I	N	I	T	I	A	L	S		S	O	L	O
F	A	K	E	S		O	P	T	I	M	A	L
I	D	E	S	T		N	A	I	V	E	T	E
C	A	S	T	S		G	R	E	E	T	E	D

In Other Words (page 152)

A	N	A		W	R	A	C	K		S	L	A	P
W	A	N	E		E	A	T	E	N		P	O	C	O
A	V	I	D		A	R	O	S	E		E	C	H	O
R	A	T	I	O	N	A	L	T	E	A	C	H	E	R
E	L	A	T	E			L	A	S	T			
			R	I	D			H	E	A	R	S
S	O	O	T		D	O	G	E		O	S	S	I	E
U	L	T	I	M	A	T	E	R	E	S	P	E	C	T
R	E	I	N	E		E	M	I	L		Y	A	K	S
A	S	S	E	T			N	I	P			
			E	R	A	S			A	R	O	M	A
L	I	B	E	R	A	L	P	R	O	M	I	S	E	R
I	R	A	N		G	O	R	E	D		S	L	A	G
S	O	S	O		E	N	A	T	E		K	E	N	O
A	N	T	S		D	E	T	E	R			R	T	S

Another Pangram (page 150)

F	A	T	B	A	C	K		A	N	T	E	S
I	D	E	A	M	E	N		M	O	U	N	T
R	E	T	S	I	N	A		A	O	R	T	A
M	A	R	S		T	V	D	I	N	N	E	R
S	L	A	V	S		E	O	N		S	N	L
			I	A	M	S	O		A	I	D	E
J	A	L	O	P	Y		Z	A	G	N	U	T
A	M	Y	L		R	H	Y	M	E			
C	P	R		A	R	B		B	L	A	K	E
Q	U	I	Z	S	H	O	W		I	N	N	S
U	L	C	E	R		M	O	M	M	I	E	S
E	L	A	T	E		B	R	A	I	L	L	E
S	A	L	A	D		S	E	X	T	E	T	S

Presidential Portraits (page 154)

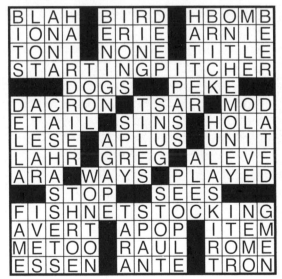

B	L	A	H		B	I	R	D		H	B	O	M	B
I	O	N	A		E	R	I	E		A	R	N	I	E
T	O	N	I		N	O	N	E		T	I	T	L	E
S	T	A	R	T	I	N	G	P	I	T	C	H	E	R
			D	O	G	S		P	E	K	E			
D	A	C	R	O	N		T	S	A	R		M	O	D
E	T	A	I	L		S	I	N	S		H	O	L	A
L	E	S	E		A	P	L	U	S		U	N	I	T
L	A	H	R		G	R	E	G		A	L	E	V	E
A	R	A		W	A	Y	S		P	L	A	Y	E	D
	S	T	O	P		S	E	E	S			
F	I	S	H	N	E	T	S	T	O	C	K	I	N	G
A	V	E	R	T		A	P	O	P		I	T	E	M
M	E	T	O	O		R	A	U	L		R	O	M	E
E	S	S	E	N		A	N	T	E		T	R	O	N

Mister Ed-ucation (page 156)

```
L E T I N   G E A R   O S L O
I T A L O   I N R I   U P O N
S T R I P   J O A N   T A G S
P A P E R D O L L S   O D I E
        O R E   E F F E C T
S T O P B Y   N O S I R
T E A R   U F O S   X A X I S
E L H I   P R O A M   N E M O
P L U M E   E N Y A   G N A W
      E R O D E   D R E A M S
Y E S M E N     A R E
I N T O   H O R S E S E N S E
E L E V   I L A Y   E M A I L
L A N E   G L U E   N I T T I
D I O R   H A L T   T R E E S
```

Watch What You Say (page 160)

```
O P T E D   B A M A   G A L S
N E A T O   F L A G   R E A L
E N D A T   L O L A   A S H E
S T A L E M A T E S   N O T E
        L E T   S T O P I T
W A F F L E   T R I A L
E L I A   T R U E   C A R P S
E E L S   S I R E S   B E E P
D E L T A   C O D A   A U R A
      A R R O W   T A R P I T
K I S S M E   W I Z
O R A L   L I P R E A D E R S
R E N E   E L I E   L E G I T
A N T E   N I N A   E N O L A
N E A P   T E A K   A S S E T
```

Dense Design (page 158)

```
L A I C   B R E L   P H I
A P S O   A U R E L I U S
S P E N D T H E N I G H T
S T E V E I R W I N
      E N S   E N C A M P
A C C R E T E   O L E O
R O O T B E E R F L O A T
A P S E   K E R N E L S
L E A R N T   C I G
      B O W D L E R I Z E
O H G O D Y O U D E V I L
O R E X E L L S   E E G S
O S T   S A L E   N Y S E
```

Triple Stackers (page 162)

```
E Y E O F T H E T I G E R
R O L L O V E R A N I R A
B U Y E R S R E M O R S E
E D A   G E E   A N T E S
      H O T W I R E
O O Z E   E P I   S O U
D O P P E L G A N G E R S
D O G   L O O   A X E S
      D I L A T O R
B I D E T   G A B   A P B
A M E R I C A N E A G L E
I N V E S T I G A T I O N
L O O K M A N O H A N D S
```

A Little California (page 164)

```
JAYWALK  BARBS
ALARMED  EQUIP
NAHUATL  LUNGE
ISON  SANTAANA
STOGY NAS MAR
 OMEGA NOME
SEXUAL CHOKED
TAFT VIPER
ERA SEN LARAM
ALCATRAZ DULE
LOTTE FIBULAS
TBONE IPANEMA
HEROD XSANDOS
```

Frequent Flier (page 168)

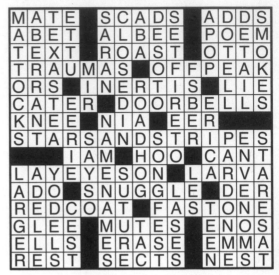

```
MATE SCADS ADDS
ABET ALBEE POEM
TEXT ROAST OTTO
TRAUMAS OFFPEAK
ORS INERTIS LIE
CATER DOORBELLS
KNEE NIA EER
STARSANDSTRIPES
 IAM HOO CANT
LAYEYESON LARVA
ADO SNUGGLE DER
REDCOAT FASTONE
GLEE MUTES ENOS
ELLS ERASE EMMA
REST SECTS NEST
```

6 × 13 (page 166)

```
ADAMSRIB ABBE
VEGGIEBURGERS
ALFREDENEUMAN
LIA NOL REEGE
 CASINOS
ZERO EEL WEE
PRINCEVALIANT
GAG EEE ODDS
 CARIBOU
CIAOS WIN DAP
INTHEPIPELINE
GRANDILOQUENT
SETS OLDTIMES
```

The Hard Stuff (page 170)

```
PEST GRASS EGOS
IDEA YALTA WANT
COPPERHEAD ELLE
ANTERO VIA OOP
SEUSS STEELTRAP
SIP ELIAS IRENE
OLLA ISM ABE
 LEADPIPECINCH
 RAS EDT DOOR
ADHOC TRIAD MAE
IRONHORSE EMIRS
SYR ARY ICANSO
LIAM GOLDDIGGER
ECCE ANISE OUST
SEEN NESTS OPTS
```